SOLIDWORKS
Sheet Metal Design 2021

CADArtifex

The premium provider of learning products and solutions
www.cadartifex.com

SOLIDWORKS Sheet Metal Design 2021

Published by
CADArtifex
www.cadartifex.com

NOTICE TO THE READER

Examination Copies

Electronic Files

Disclaimer

www.cadartifex.com

Dedication

First and foremost, I would like to thank my parents for being a great support throughout my career and while writing this book.

Heartfelt gratitude goes to my wife and my sisters for their patience and endurance in supporting me to take up and successfully accomplish this challenge.

I would also like to acknowledge the efforts of the employees at CADArtifex for their dedication in editing the content of this textbook.

Table of Contents

Preface

SOLIDWORKS, developed by Dassault Systèmes SOLIDWORKS Corp., world leader in engineering software, offers a complete set of 3D software tools that let you create, simulate, publish, and manage your data. By providing advanced solid modeling techniques, SOLIDWORKS helps engineers to optimize performance while designing with capabilities, that cut down on costly prototypes, and eliminate rework and delays, thereby saving time as well as development costs.

SOLIDWORKS is a feature-based, parametric solid-modeling mechanical design and automation software which allows you to convert 2D sketches into 3D models by using simple but highly effective modeling tools. The 3D components and assemblies created in SOLIDWORKS can be converted into 2D drawings within a few mouse clicks. In addition, you can validate your designs by simulating their real-world conditions and assessing the environmental impact of products.

SOLIDWORKS Sheet Metal Design 2021 textbook has been designed for instructor-led courses as well as self-paced learning. It is intended to help engineers and designers interested in learning SOLIDWORKS for creating real-world sheet metal components. This textbook is a great help for SOLIDWORKS users new to sheet metal design. It consists of total 132 pages covering the sheet metal design environment of SOLIDWORKS. It teaches users to use SOLIDWORKS mechanical design software for creating parametric 3D sheet metal components.

This textbook not only focuses on the usage of the tools and commands of SOLIDWORKS for creating sheet metal components but also on the concept of design. It contains Tutorials followed by theory that provide users with step-by-step instructions for creating sheet metal components. Moreover, it ends with Hands-on Test Drives which allow users to experience the user friendly and technical capabilities of SOLIDWORKS.

Prerequisites

You should be familiar with SOLIDWORKS user interface and the basics of creating 3D solid parts. You can refer to **SOLIDWORKS 2021: A Power Guide for Beginners and Intermediate Users** textbook by **CADArtifex** for learning different design techniques of creating 3D solid parts, assemblies, and 2D drawings.

What Is Covered in This Textbook

SOLIDWORKS Sheet Metal Design 2021 textbook is designed to help you understand everything you need to know to start using SOLIDWORKS 2021 for creating real-world **sheet metal components**.

Who Should Read This Textbook

This textbook is written with a wide range of SOLIDWORKS users in mind, varying from beginners to advanced users as well as SOLIDWORKS instructors interested in learning sheet metal designs. The easy-to-follow instructions of this textbook allow you to clearly understand different design techniques, SOLIDWORKS sheet metal design tools, and design principles.

Icons/Terms used in This Textbook

The following icons and terms are used in this textbook:

Note

Note: Notes highlight information requiring special attention.

Tip

Tip: Tips provide additional advice, which increases the efficiency of the users.

Flyout

A Flyout is a list in which a set of tools are grouped together, see Figure 1.

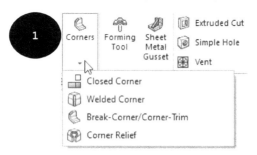

Drop-down List

A drop-down list is a list in which a set of options is grouped together, see Figure 2.

Rollout

A rollout is an area in which drop-down list, fields, buttons, check boxes are available to specify various parameters, see Figure 2. A rollout can either be in expanded or in collapsed form. You can expand/collapse a rollout by clicking on the arrow available on the right of its title bar.

Field

A Field allows you to enter new value, or modify an existing/default value, as per your requirement, see Figure 2. Also, a field allows you to select entities from the graphics area.

Check box

A Check box allows you to turn on or off the functions of a particular option, see Figure 2.

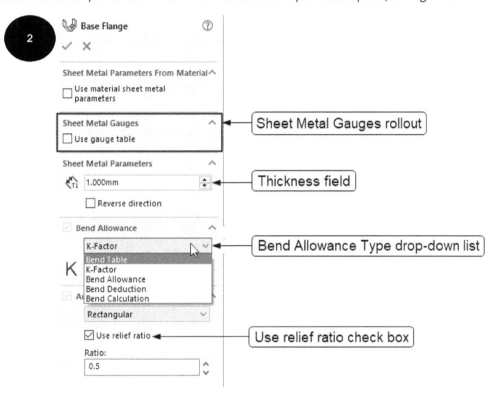

How to Get Access to Online Resources

Students and faculty members can get access to all parts used in the illustrations, Tutorials and Hand-on Test Drives of the textbook. In addition, faculty can also get access to PowerPoint Presentations (PPT).

To get complete access to the online resources of this textbook, write to us at *info@cadartifex.com*, highlighting the name of the textbook and ISBN. The resources will be shared with you via email.

How to Contact the Author

We value your feedback and suggestions. Please email us at *info@cadartifex.com* for any assistnace.

We thank you for purchasing **SOLIDWORKS Sheet Metal Design 2021** textbook. We hope that the information and concepts introduced in this textbook help you to accomplish your professional goals.

Creating Sheet Metal Components

In this book, the following topics will be discussed:

- Installing SOLIDWORKS
- Getting Started with SOLIDWORKS
- Invoking the Part Modeling Environment
- Getting Started with Sheet Metal Design
- Creating a Base Flange
- Understanding Nodes of FeatureManager Design Tree
- Creating an Edge Flange
- Creating a Tab Feature
- Creating a Miter Flange
- Creating a Sketched Bend
- Creating a Jog Bend
- Creating a Hem Feature
- Closing Corners
- Welding Corners
- Breaking Corners
- Adding Corner Reliefs
- Creating a Lofted Bend
- Creating an Extruded Cut Feature
- Creating a Forming Tool
- Inserting a Forming Tool
- Creating a Vent
- Converting a 3D Solid Part into a Sheet Metal
- Converting a 3D Shelled Part into a Sheet Metal
- Mirroring and Patterning a Sheet Metal Feature
- Creating a Flat Pattern of a Sheet Metal Part
- Flattening Selected Bends of a Sheet Metal Part
- Folding Selected Bends of a Sheet Metal Part
- Creating Cuts Across the Bends
- Defining Sheet Parameters to a Custom Material
- Customizing the CommandManager
- Generating a Drawing View of the Flat Pattern

Welcome to the world of Computer Aided Design (CAD) with SOLIDWORKS. SOLIDWORKS, a product of Dassault Systèmes SOLIDWORKS Corp., world leader in engineering software, offers a complete set of 3D software tools that lets you create, simulate, publish, and manage your data. By providing advanced solid modeling techniques, SOLIDWORKS helps engineers to optimize performance while designing with capabilities, that cut down on costly prototypes and eliminate rework and delays, thereby saving time as well as development costs.

SOLIDWORKS is a feature-based, parametric solid-modeling mechanical design and automation software which allows you to convert 2D sketches into solid models by using simple but highly effective modeling tools. SOLIDWORKS provides a wide range of tools that allow you to create real-world components and assemblies. These real-world components and assemblies can then be converted into 2D engineering drawings for production. In addition, you can validate your designs by simulating their real-world conditions and assessing the environmental impact of products.

SOLIDWORKS utilizes a parametric feature-based approach for creating models. With SOLIDWORKS you can share your designs with your partners, subcontractors and colleagues in smart new ways, which improves knowledge transfer and shortens the design cycle.

Installing SOLIDWORKS

If you do not have SOLIDWORKS installed on your system, you first need to get it installed. However, before you start installing SOLIDWORKS, you need to evaluate the system requirements and ensure that you have a system capable of running SOLIDWORKS adequately. Below are the system requirements for installing SOLIDWORKS 2021.

1.   Operating Systems: Windows 10 - 64-bit
2.   RAM: 8 GB or more (16 GB or more recommended)
3.   Disk Space: 10 GB or more
4.   Processor: 3.3 GHz or higher
5.   Graphics Card: SOLIDWORKS certified graphics cards and drivers

For more information about the system requirements for SOLIDWORKS, visit the SOLIDWORKS website at *https://www.solidworks.com/sw/support/SystemRequirements.html*

Once the system is ready, install SOLIDWORKS by using the SOLIDWORKS DVD or by using the downloaded SOLIDWORKS setup files.

Getting Started with SOLIDWORKS

Once SOLIDWORKS 2021 is installed on your system, start SOLIDWORKS 2021 by double-clicking on the **SOLIDWORKS 2021** icon on the desktop of your system. As soon as you double-click on the SOLIDWORKS 2021 icon, the system prepares for starting SOLIDWORKS by loading all required files. Once all the required files have been loaded, the startup user interface of SOLIDWORKS 2021 appears along with the **Welcome** dialog box, see Figure 1. If you are starting SOLIDWORKS for the first time after installing the software, the **SOLIDWORKS License Agreement** window appears, see Figure 2. Click on the **Accept** button in the **SOLIDWORKS License Agreement** window to accept the license agreement and start SOLIDWORKS 2021.

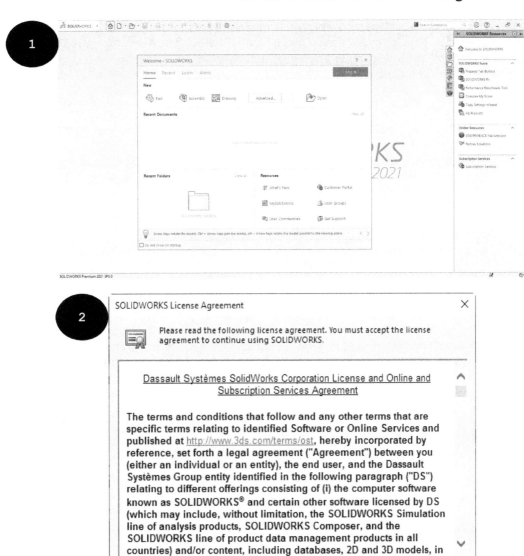

In SOLIDWORKS, the **Welcome** dialog box appears every time you start SOLIDWORKS and provides a convenient way to invoke new SOLIDWORKS documents, open existing documents, view recent documents and folders, access SOLIDWORKS resources, and stay updated on SOLIDWORKS news.

The **Welcome** dialog box has four tabs: **Home**, **Recent**, **Learn**, and **Alerts**. The options in the **Home** tab are used for invoking new SOLIDWORKS documents (**Part**, **Assembly**, and **Drawing**), opening existing documents, viewing recent documents and folder, and accessing SOLIDWORKS resources. The **Recent** tab displays a list of recent documents and folders. The **Learn** tab is used for accessing instructional resources such as tutorials, sample models, access to 3D Content Center, certification program, and so on to help you learn more about SOLIDWORKS. The **Alerts** tab is used for updating you with SOLIDWORKS news and provides different types of alerts in different sections including **Troubleshooting** and **Technical Alerts**.

Tip: If the **Welcome** dialog box does not appear on the screen, then you can invoke it by clicking on the **Welcome to SOLIDWORKS** tool 🏠 in the **Standard** toolbar or by pressing the CTRL + F2 keys. Alternatively, you can click on **Help > Welcome to SOLIDWORKS** in the SOLIDWORKS Menus or the **Welcome to SOLIDWORKS** option in the **SOLIDWORKS Resources Task Pane** to invoke the **Welcome** dialog box. You will learn more about **Standard** toolbar, SOLIDWORKS Menus, and **SOLIDWORKS Resources Task Pane** later.

In SOLIDWORKS, you can create Sheet Metal components within the Part modeling environment, therefore it is important to first get familiar with different components of the Part modeling environment. The method for invoking the Part modeling environment is discussed next.

Invoking the Part Modeling Environment

To invoke the Part modeling environment, click on the **Part** button in the **Welcome** dialog box. The Part modeling environment gets invoked and the startup user interface of the Part modeling environment appears, as shown in Figure 3. Alternatively, to invoke the Part modeling environment, click on the **New** tool in the **Standard** toolbar, see Figure 4. The **New SOLIDWORKS Document** dialog box appears. In this dialog box, make sure that the **Part** button is activated and then click on the **OK** button.

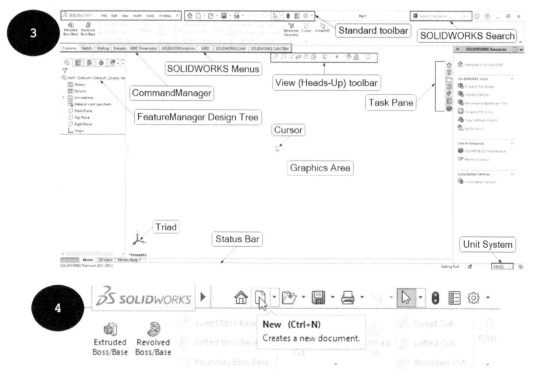

Note: If you are invoking the Part modeling environment for the first time after installing the software, the **Units and Dimension Standard** dialog box appears, see Figure 5. In this dialog box, you can specify the default unit system for SOLIDWORKS documents.

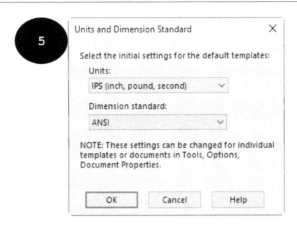

Tip: Similar to invoking the Part modeling environment for creating parts/components, you can invoke the Assembly environment for creating assemblies and the Drawing environment for creating 2D drawings by using the Assembly and Drawing buttons of the Welcome dialog box, respectively.

Some of the components of the startup user interface of the Part modeling environment are discussed next.

Standard Toolbar

The **Standard** toolbar contains a set of the most frequently used tools such as **New**, **Open**, and **Save**, see Figure 6.

SOLIDWORKS Menus

The SOLIDWORKS Menus contains different menus such as **File**, **View**, and **Tools** for accessing different tools of SOLIDWORKS, see Figure 7.

Note that the SOLIDWORKS Menus appears when you move the cursor on the SOLIDWORKS logo, which is available at the top left corner of the screen. You can keep the SOLIDWORKS Menus visible all the time by clicking on the push-pin button ✗ available at the end of the SOLIDWORKS Menus. Note that the tools in the different menus are dependent upon the type of environment invoked.

SOLIDWORKS Search

The SOLIDWORKS Search is a search tool for searching commands/tools, knowledge base (help topics), community forum, files, models, and so on, see Figure 8.

CommandManager

CommandManager is available at the top of the graphics area. It provides access to different sets of SOLIDWORKS tools. There are various CommandManagers such as **Features CommandManager**, **Sketch CommandManager**, **Sheet Metal CommandManager**, and **Evaluate CommandManager** available in the Part modeling environment. You can access these CommandManagers by clicking on their respective tabs. On clicking the **Features** tab, the **Features CommandManager** appears, which provides access to various tools for creating a 3D solid component, see Figures 9 and 10. Figure 9 shows the partial view of the **Features CommandManager** and Figure 10 shows a 3D solid component created by creating all its features one by one by using the solid modeling tools.

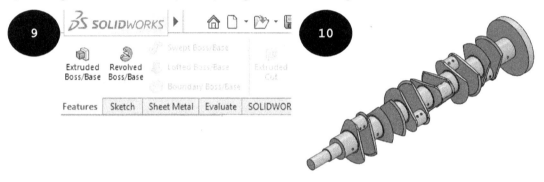

Note: To learn creating 3D solid components, assemblies, and 2D drawings, refer to **SOLIDWORKS 2021: A Power Guide for Beginners and Intermediate User** textbook by CADArtifex.

Similarly, on clicking the **Sheet Metal** tab, the **Sheet Metal CommandManager** appears, which provides access to various tools for creating a sheet metal component, see Figures 11 and 12. Figure 11 shows the partial view of the **Sheet Metal CommandManager** and Figure 12 shows a sheet metal component. If the **Sheet Metal** tab is not available in the CommandManager, then you need to customize to add it. You will learn more about adding the **Sheet Metal CommandManager** and its tool later.

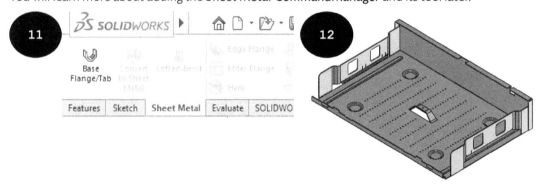

Tip: The different environments (Part, Assembly, and Drawing) of SOLIDWORKS are provided with different sets of CommandManagers.

FeatureManager Design Tree

FeatureManager Design Tree appears on the left of the graphics area and keeps a record of all operations or features used for creating a model, see Figure 13. Note that the first created feature appears at the top and the next created features appear one after the other in the FeatureManager Design Tree. Also, in the FeatureManager Design Tree, three default planes and an origin appear, by default.

Tip: The features are logical operations that are performed to create a component. In other words, a component can be designed by creating a number of features.

View (Heads-Up) Toolbar

The View (Heads-Up) toolbar is available at the top center of the graphics area, see Figure 14. It is provided with different sets of tools that are used for manipulating the view and display of a model available in the graphics area.

Status Bar

The Status Bar is available at the bottom of the graphics area and provides information about the action to be taken based on the currently active tool. It also displays the current state of the sketch being created, coordinate system, and so on.

Task Pane

Task Pane appears on the right side of the screen with various tabs such as **SOLIDWORKS Resources**, **Design Library**, **File Explorer**, **Appearances, Scenes, and Decals**, and **Custom Properties** for accessing various online resources of SOLIDWORKS, several applications, subscription services, library, and so on, see Figure 15.

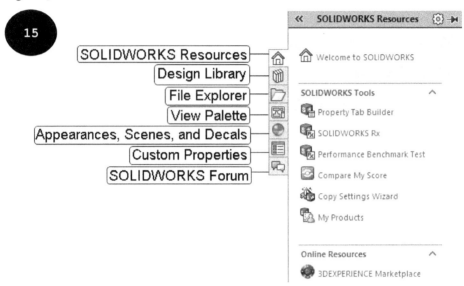

Getting Started with Sheet Metal Design

As discussed earlier, you can create sheet metal components within the Part modeling environment by using various tools available in the **Sheet Metal CommandManager**. To display the tools of the **Sheet Metal CommandManager**, click on the **Sheet Metal** tab in the CommandManager, see Figure 16.

If the **Sheet Metal** tab is not available in the CommandManager then right-click anywhere on the CommandManager. Next, click on the **Tabs > Sheet Metal** option in the shortcut menu that appears, see Figure 17. The **Sheet Metal** tab becomes available in the CommandManager. Note that initially, most of the tools of the **Sheet Metal CommandManager** are not activated. These tools get activated as soon as you create a base flange of a sheet metal component.

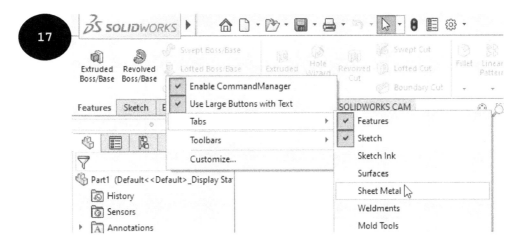

Note: In the shortcut menu shown in Figure 17, a tick-mark in front of the CommandManager name indicates that the respective CommandManager is already added. You can add any CommandManager that is not available by default, on clicking its name.

A sheet metal component is a thin and flat piece of metal that has a uniform thickness ranging from 0.154 mm (0.006 in) to 6.35 mm (0.25 in). A sheet metal component is created by performing a range of techniques, including bending, cutting, and drawing on a sheet, see below table.

Techniques	Types	Illustration	Description
Bending	V-bending	F Punch Sheet Die	V-bending is a bending process in which the punch pushes the sheet into a V-shaped groove of the die causing it to bend.
	Edge bending	Sheet Pressure pad F Punch Die	Edge bending is a process in which the punch pushes the sheet that extends beyond the die and pad, against the edge the die causing it to bend.

Cutting	Shearing		Shearing is a cutting process in which the sheet is divided or cut into two parts by applying a great enough shearing force on the sheet, against the edge of the die, using the punch.
	Blanking		Blanking is a process in which a piece of sheet is removed from a large stock. This removed piece is also called blank and is not scrap, rather a desired part that will be used for further processing.
	Punching		Punching is a cutting process in which a piece of sheet is removed from a large stock and creates a hole on the sheet. The removed piece is scrap.

| Drawing | Drawing (Before and After operations) | 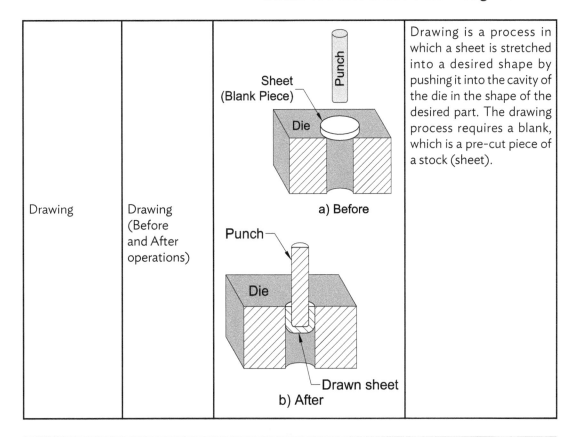 a) Before b) After | Drawing is a process in which a sheet is stretched into a desired shape by pushing it into the cavity of the die in the shape of the desired part. The drawing process requires a blank, which is a pre-cut piece of a stock (sheet). |

Tip: An extremely thin metal whose thickness is less than 0.154 mm (0.006 in) is known as a foil and a thicker metal whose thickness is greater than 6.35 mm (0.25 in) is known as a plate.

It is evident from the above table that in the tool room or a machine shop, you need to perform various operations such as bending, cutting, and drawing on a flat sheet of uniform thickness for creating a sheet metal component of a desired shape, see Figure 18. To create a sheet metal component, the most important thing that you need before creating it is the flat pattern layout of the component, see Figure 19. It provides the flattened view of the sheet metal component. Figure 18 shows a sheet metal component and Figure 19 shows its flat pattern layout.

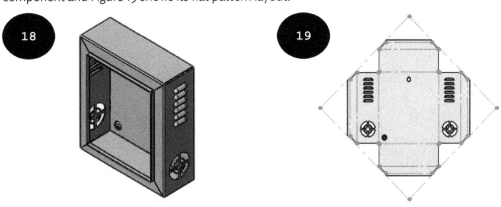

In SOLIDWORKS, you can create a sheet metal component by using various tools of the **Sheet Metal CommandManager** and then generate its flat pattern layout with a single click. To create a sheet metal component, you need to create all its features one by one, see Figure 20. The first created feature of a sheet metal component is known as the base flange. Figure 20 depicts the process for creating a sheet metal component and Figure 21 shows its flat pattern.

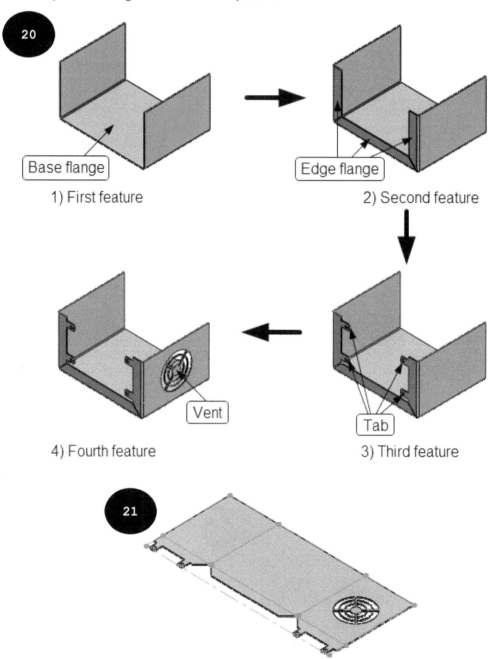

20

Base flange

1) First feature

Edge flange

2) Second feature

Vent

4) Fourth feature

Tab

3) Third feature

21

Note that the sheet metal parameters such as material thickness, bend radius, and bend allowance are defined while creating the base flange and the same are used for all the remaining flanges or features of the sheet metal component as the default parameters. These sheet metal parameters are used for calculating the total flattened length of the sheet metal component.

Creating a Base Flange

The first created feature of a sheet metal component is known as the base flange. You can create a base flange by using an open or a closed sketch, see Figures 22 and 23.

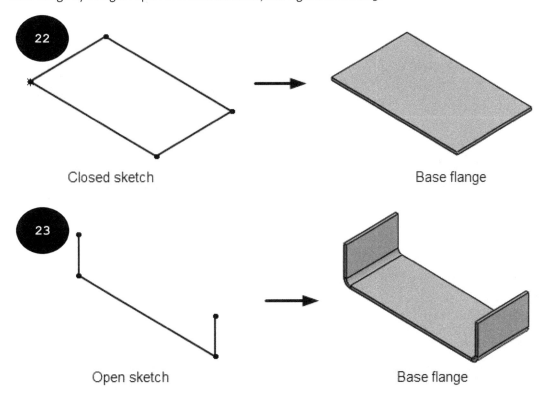

Closed sketch   Base flange

Open sketch   Base flange

To create a base flange, invoke the Sketching environment and then create an open sketch or a closed sketch by using the sketching tools.

Tip: To invoke the Sketching environment, click on the **Sketch** tool in the **Sketch CommandManager** and then select a plane as the sketching plane for creating the sketch of the base flange. Refer to **SOLIDWORKS 2021: A Power Guide for Beginners and Intermediate User** textbook by CADArtifex to learn about creating sketches, 3D solid components, assemblies, and 2D drawings.

After creating a sketch, click on the **Sheet Metal** tab in the CommandManager and then click on the **Base Flange/Tab** tool, see Figure 24. The **Base Flange PropertyManager** appears, see Figure 25. Also, the preview of the base flange as per the default sheet metal parameters appears in the graphics area, see Figure 26. Note that the **Direction 1** and **Direction 2** rollout of the PropertyManager are available only if the sketch of the base flange is an open sketch. The options in the **Base Flange PropertyManager** are used for defining the sheet metal parameters such as material thickness, bend radius, and bend allowance, which are also used as default parameters for the entire sheet metal component. However, you can edit these default parameters at any point in time of the designing process. You will learn about editing the default parameters of the sheet metal component later. The options in the **Base Flange PropertyManager** are discussed next.

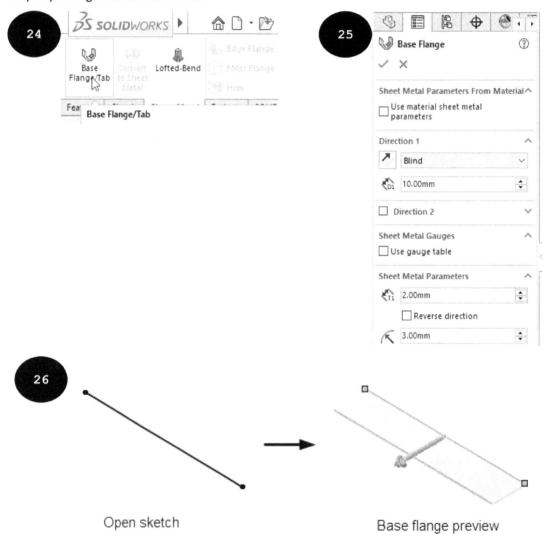

Open sketch

Base flange preview

Note: If you exit the Sketching environment after creating the sketch and the sketch is not selected in the graphics area, then on invoking the **Base Flange/Tab** tool, the **Message PropertyManager** appears and you are prompted to select either a sketch or a sketching plane. Select the sketch in the graphics area. The **Base Flange PropertyManager** and the preview of the base flange appear. However, if the sketch is not created then you can select a sketching plane for creating the sketch in the Sketching environment.

Use material sheet metal parameters

On selecting the **Use material sheet metal parameters** check box, the sheet metal parameters that are defined with the assigned custom material of the current part document will be used for the sheet metal component being created. If a material is not defined to the current part document then on selecting this check box, a message appears that "**There is no material applied to the part**". Also, if a material is defined without the sheet metal parameters, then on selecting this check box, a message appears that "**There are no valid sheet metal parameters defined with the material**". You will learn about defining sheet metal parameters to a custom material of a part document later.

Direction 1

The options in the **Direction 1** rollout of the PropertyManager are used for defining the end condition or termination of the base flange in one direction. Note that this rollout is available only if the sketch of the base flange is an open sketch.

> **Tip:** If the **Direction 1** rollout is in collapse form, you need to expand it by clicking on the arrow available in its title bar for displaying its options.

By default, the **Blind** option is selected in the **End Condition** drop-down list of the **Direction 1** rollout. As a result, you can specify the end condition of the base flange in one direction by specifying its depth value in the **Depth** field of the rollout, see Figure 27. The **Reverse Direction** button is used to flip the direction of extrusion to either side of the sketching plane.

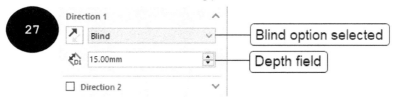

The **Mid Plane** option in the **End Condition** drop-down list is used for extruding the base flange symmetrically about the sketching plane. The **Up To Vertex, Up To Surface**, and **Offset From Surface** options of the drop-down list are used for extruding the base flange up to a selected vertex, surface, and at an offset distance from a selected surface, respectively. Note that these options are used while creating the second and further flanges of a sheet metal component.

Direction 2

The options in the **Direction 2** rollout are same as those in the **Direction 1** rollout of the PropertyManager with the only difference that the options of the **Direction 2** rollout are used for specifying the end condition of the base flange in the second direction of the sketching plane.

> **Note:** As discussed earlier, the **Direction 1** and **Direction 2** rollouts of the PropertyManager are available only if the sketch of the base flange is an open sketch.

Sheet Metal Gauges

In SOLIDWORKS, you can select a gauge table with pre-defined sheet metal parameters for creating a sheet metal component. A gauge table is simply a Microsoft Excel spreadsheet, which enables you to choose an appropriate sheet metal thickness, base on the material and the gauge numbers. A gauge number refers to the standard thickness of a sheet metal and typically is in the range from 3 to 38. The higher the gauge number, thinner will be the sheet metal thickness. A gauge table also contains a list of available bend radii, based on the thickness of the sheet metal and the available tooling to be used in the bending process. It limits the choices that the designers have for selecting a bend radius based on availability. Moreover, a gauge table contains the appropriate K-factor for calculating the bend allowance, which represents the stretch of the sheet metal in the bent regions, see Figure 28. Alternatively, it can contain the calculated bend allowance or bend deduction values to represent the stretch of sheet metal in the bend regions for calculating the total flat length of the sheet, refer to Figures 28 and 29. Figures 28 illustrates the concept of the bend allowance for calculating the flat length of sheet metal.

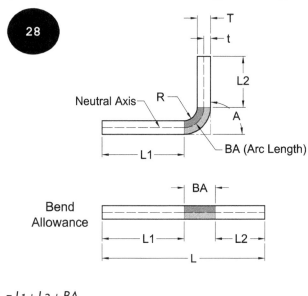

$L = L_1 + L_2 + BA$

Where,

L = Total flat length
L_1 = Leg length 1
L_2 = Leg length 2
BA = Bend allowance

Bend allowance (BA) $= A\,(\pi/180)\,(R + (K \times T))$

Where,

A = Bend angle
R = Inside bend radius
K = K-factor
T = Material Thickness

K-factor (K) = t / T

Where,

T = *Material Thickness*
t = *Distance from the neutral axis to the inside face*

Note: The K-factor is defined as the ratio between the distance from the neutral axis to the inner bend face and the material thickness. Note that when a sheet is bent, its inner portion gets compressed and its outer portion gets expanded/stretched. The line where the transition from the compression to the expansion occurs is known as the neutral axis, refer to Figures 28 and 29. The original position of the neutral axis is at 50 percent (center) of the material thickness of a flat sheet. However, when bending the sheet, the position of the neutral axis gets shifted towards the inner face of the bend and it varies depending on the bend angle, bend radius, material properties, and the method of bending.

Figure 29 illustrates the concept of bend deduction for calculating the flat length of sheet metal.

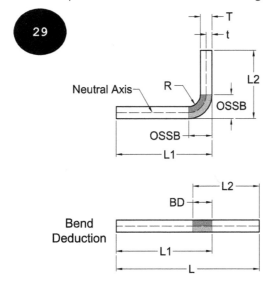

L = L1 + L2 - BD

Where,

L = *Total flat length*
L1 = *Leg length 1*
L2 = *Leg length 2*
BD = *Bend deduction*

Bend deduction (BD) = (2 X OSSB) - BA

Where,

OSSB = *Outside setback*
BA = *Bend allowance*

$$\text{Outside setback (OSSB)} = (R + T)\ \text{Tan } A/2$$

Where,

R = Inside bend radius
T = Material Thickness
A = Bend angle

To select a gauge table with pre-defined sheet metal parameters, select the **Use gauge table** check box in the **Sheet Metal Gauges** rollout of the PropertyManager. The **Select Table** drop-down list is enabled below this check box. This drop-down list displays a list of all the available gauge tables, see Figure 30. Select the required gauge table in this drop-down list. Figure 31 shows the default "SAMPLE TABLE - ALUMINUM - METRIC UNITS" gauge table. In this table, the gauge numbers are available in the range from 10 and 26. Also, each gauge number represent a standard thickness and the available bend radius. Also, in this gauge table, the K-factor is considered as 0.5.

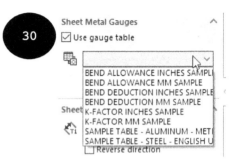

Figure 32 shows an upper portion of the default "**BEND ALLOWANCE MM SAMPLE**" gauge table. In this table, the available gauge numbers are 3, 4, and 5. Also, the calculated bend allowance is defined corresponding to the bend angle and the bend radius. For example, the bend allowance corresponding to the bend angle 90 degrees and the bend radius 3 mm is defined as 0.27 mm in case of gauge 5.

	A	B	C
1			
2	Type:	Aluminum Gauge Table	
3	Process	Aluminum - Coining	
4	K-Factor	0.5	
5	Unit:	millimeters	
6			
7	Gauge No.	Gauge (Thickness)	Available Bend Radius
8	Gauge 10	3	3.0; 4.0; 5.0; 8.0; 10.0
9	Gauge 12	2.5	3.0; 4.0; 5.0; 8.0; 10.0
10	Gauge 14	2	2.0; 3.0; 4.0; 5.0; 8.0; 10.0
11	Gauge 16	1.5	1.5; 2.0; 3.0; 4.0; 5.0; 8.0; 10.0
12	Gauge 18	1.2	1.5; 2.0; 3.0; 4.0; 5.0; 8.0; 10.0
13	Gauge 20	0.9	1.0; 1.5; 2.0; 3.0; 4.0; 5.0
14	Gauge 22	0.7	0.8; 1.0; 1.5; 2.0; 3.0; 4.0; 5.0
15	Gauge 24	0.6	0.8; 1.0; 1.5; 2.0; 3.0; 4.0; 5.0
16	Gauge 26	0.5	0.5; 0.8; 1.0; 1.5; 2.0; 3.0; 4.0; 5.0
17			

32

	A	B	C	D	E	F
1	**Type:**	Steel Gauge Table				
2	**Process**	Steel Air Bending				
3	**Bend Type:**	Bend Allowance				
4	**Unit:**	millimeters				
5	**Material:**	Steel				
6						
7	**Gauge No.**	**Gauge 5**				
8	**Thickness:**	**1**				
9	**Angle**		**Radius**			
10			1.00	2.00	3.00	4.00
11	15		0.25	0.26	0.27	0.28
12	30		0.25	0.26	0.27	0.28
13	45		0.25	0.26	0.27	0.28
14	60		0.25	0.26	0.27	0.28
15	75		0.25	0.26	0.27	0.28
16	90		0.25	0.26	0.27	0.28
17						
18	**Gauge No.**	**Gauge 4**				
19	**Thickness:**	**1.5**				
20	**Angle**		**Radius**			
21			1.00	2.00	3.00	4.00
22	15		0.30	0.31	0.32	0.33
23	30		0.30	0.31	0.32	0.33
24	45		0.30	0.31	0.32	0.33
25	60		0.30	0.31	0.32	0.33
26	75		0.30	0.31	0.32	0.33
27	90		0.30	0.31	0.32	0.33
28						

In SOLIDWORKS, you can edit the parameters of a default gauge table or create a new gauge table in the Microsoft Excel spreadsheet. For doing so, browse to *C:\Program Files\SOLIDWORKS Corp\ SOLIDWORKS\lang\english\Sheet Metal Gauge Tables* location in the installation directory of your system, see Figure 33. Next, double-click on an existing gauge table to open it as a Microsoft Excel spreadsheet and then edit its properties, as required. Next, save the modified gauge table with new name in the **Sheet Metal Gauge Tables** folder at the same location. Note that the Microsoft Excel spreadsheet files that are saved in the **Sheet Metal Gauge Tables** folder are displayed in the **Select Table** drop-down list of the **Sheet Metal Gauges** rollout in the PropertyManager as gauge tables.

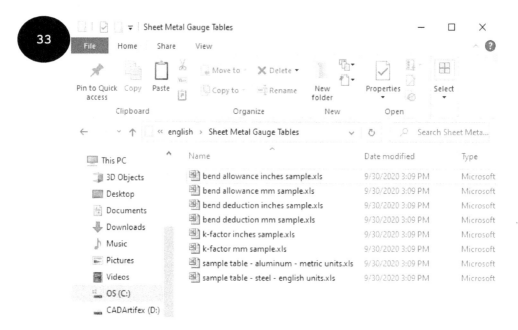

After selecting a gauge table in the **Select Table** drop-down list of the **Sheet Metal Gauges** rollout in the PropertyManager, the options for defining the material thickness, bend radius, and bend allowance becomes available in their respective drop-down lists of the PropertyManager, see Figure 34. The availability of these options depends upon the data specified in the selected gauge table. Select the required option to define the material thickness in term of a gauge number and the bend radius of the sheet in their respective drop-down list. Also, the **Bend Calculation** option is selected in the **Bend Allowance Type** drop-down list, by default. As a result, the value for calculating the flat length of the sheet metal in terms of bend allowance, bend deduction, or K-factor is imported from the selected gauge table. You can select any other option in the **Bend Allowance Type** drop-down list to manually define the respective value for calculating the flat length of the sheet.

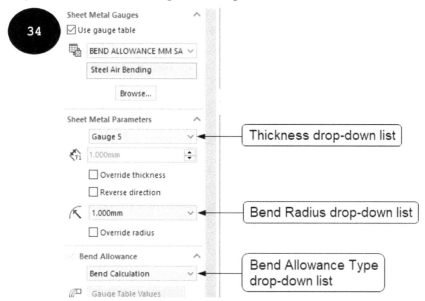

Note: The selection of a gauge table, limits the choice that the designers have for defining the sheet metal thickness and the bend radius based on the availability. However, you can override the thickness and bend radius values by selecting the **Override thickness** and **Override radius** check boxes in the **Sheet Metal Parameters** rollout, respectively.

Tip: Without using a gauge table, you can define the sheet metal parameters, manually in the **Sheet Metal Parameters** and **Bend Allowance** rollouts of the PropertyManager.

Sheet Metal Parameters

The options in the **Sheet Metal Parameters** rollout are used for defining the material thickness and the bend radius, see Figure 35. The options are discussed next.

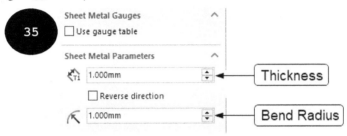

Note: The availability of options in the **Sheet Metal Parameters** rollout for defining the sheet metal thickness and bend radius depends on whether a gauge table is selected or not. Figure 35 shows the **Sheet Metal Parameters** rollout when a gauge table is not selected.

Thickness

The **Thickness** field of the **Sheet Metal Parameters** rollout is used for specifying a uniform thickness for the sheet metal component to be created.

Bend Radius

The **Bend Radius** field is used for specifying a default bend radius for the sheet metal. You can enter a bend radius in this field, based on the thickness of the sheet metal and the available tooling to be used in the bending process, refer to Figure 36. In this figure, a typical punch and die set is used for bending a sheet of uniform thickness. Note that the punch and die have a radius at their peak, and these radii cause a specific bend radius in the sheet metal when forming a bend in the bending process.

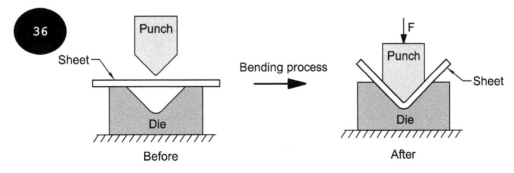

Reverse direction

The **Reverse direction** check box is used to flip the direction of material thickness to the other side of the sketch in the graphics area.

Bend Allowance

The **Bend Allowance Type** drop-down list in the **Bend Allowance** rollout is used for selecting an option to define the bend allowance, which represents the stretch of the sheet metal in the bent regions. Figure 37 shows the expanded **Bend Allowance Type** drop-down list. The options in this drop-down list are discussed next.

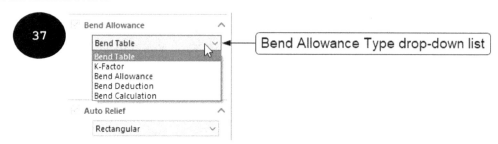

Bend Table

The **Bend Table** option is used for selecting a bend table, which is simply a Microsoft Excel spreadsheet for defining the bend allowance of the sheet metal. On selecting this option, the **Bend Table** drop-down list becomes available in the rollout with a list of all the available bend tables, see Figure 38. In this figure, a list of default bend tables are displayed in the drop-down list.

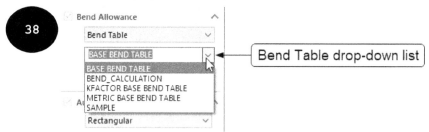

Note: A bend table contains calculated bend allowance or bend deduction values corresponding to thickness, bend angle, and bend radius values. Alternatively, it can contain K-Factor values for calculating the bend allowance of the sheet metal.

Select the required bend table in the **Bend Table** drop-down list for defining the bend allowance, bend deduction, or K-factor value, respectively as per the specified thickness and bend radius. It is also depends upon the bend angle of the sheet metal.

Note: You can edit a default bend table or create a new bend table in the Microsoft Excel spreadsheet. To do so, browse to *C:\Program Files\SOLIDWORKS Corp\SOLIDWORKS\lang\ english\Sheetmetal Bend Tables* location in the installation directory of your system. Next, double-click on an existing bend table to open it as a Microsoft Excel spreadsheet and then edit its properties or enter new properties, as required. Next, save the modified bend table with a new name in the **Sheetmetal Bend Tables** folder at the same location. Note that the Microsoft Excel spreadsheet files that are saved in the **Sheetmetal Bend Tables** folder are displayed in the **Bend Table** drop-down list as bend tables. In addition to the Microsoft Excel file, a bend table can also be created as a text file with *.btl* file extension.

K-Factor

On selecting the **K-Factor** option in the **Bend Allowance Type** drop-down list, you need to manually enter the required K-factor value in the field that appears below the drop-down list, see Figure 39. The concept of K-Factor is discussed earlier under the heading **Sheet Metal Gauges**.

Note: The concept of bend allowance, bend deduction, and K-Factor is discussed earlier with illustrations discussing the topic **Sheet Metal Gauges**, refer to page 26.

Bend Allowance

On selecting the **Bend Allowance** option, you need to manually enter the bend allowance value in the field that appears below the drop-down list, see Figure 40.

Bend Deduction

On selecting the **Bend Deduction** option in the **Bend Allowance Type** drop-down list, you need to manually enter the bend deduction value in the field that appears below the drop-down list.

Bend Calculation

On selecting the **Bend Calculation** option, the bend allowance, bend deduction, or K-factor value gets imported from the table selected in the drop-down list that appears below the **Bend Allowance Type** drop-down list.

Auto Relief

The **Auto Relief Type** drop-down list in the **Auto Relief** rollout is used for selecting a relief type (rectangular, tear, or obround) to be added automatically in bend regions for preventing or avoiding the unwanted deformation or tear in the sheet metal. Figure 41 shows the options in the **Auto Relief Type** drop-down list and the same are discussed next.

Rectangular

The **Rectangular** option is used for adding rectangular relief cuts in the bend regions of a sheet, refer to Figure 42. When you select this option, you need to define the width and depth values of the rectangular relief cut. By default, the **Use relief ratio** check box is selected in the **Auto Relief** rollout. As a result, the relief ratio is used for calculating the width and depth values of the relief cut. You can enter the relief ratio in the range from 0.05 to 2.0 in the **Relief Ratio** field of the rollout. The higher the value of relief ratio, the larger the size (depth and width) of the relief cut added in the bend region. The equations for calculating the width and depth values by using the relief ratio are given below:

Width value = Relief ratio x Material Thickness

Depth value = Relief ratio x Material Thickness

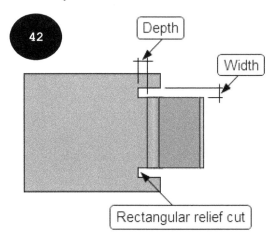

You can also enter the required width and depth values directly in the **Relief Width** and **Relief Depth** fields that appear when the **Use relief ratio** check box is cleared in the **Auto Relief** rollout of the PropertyManager, see Figure 43.

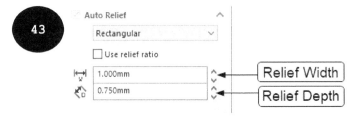

Note: In Figure 42, an edge flange is created at an angle on an existing edge of the sheet with rectangular relief cut. You will learn more about creating edge flange and the application of adding reliefs in the bends later.

Tear

The **Tear** option is used for adding tear relief cuts in the bend regions of the sheet, refer to Figure 44. A tear relief is simply a face-to-face shear of the material with no gap. It requires a minimum size for inserting the bend in the sheet. In SOLIDWORKS, you can add two types of tear relief cuts: **Rip** and **Extend**. You will learn about both these types of tear reliefs later.

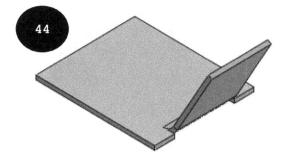

Obround

The **Obround** option is used for adding obround relief cuts in the bend regions of a sheet, refer to Figure 45. When you select this option, you need to define the width and depth values of the obround relief cut. By default, the **Use relief ratio** check box is selected in the **Auto Relief** rollout. As a result, the relief ratio is used for calculating the width and depth values of the relief cut. You can enter the relief ratio in the range from 0.05 to 2.0 in the **Relief Ratio** field of the rollout. The higher the value of relief ratio, the larger the size (depth and width) of the relief cut added in the bend region. The equations for calculating the width and depth values by using the relief ratio are the same as discussed earlier while creating the rectangular relief cut.

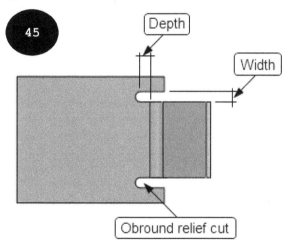

You can also enter the required width and depth values directly in the **Relief Width** and **Relief Depth** fields that appear when the **Use relief ratio** check box is cleared in the **Auto Relief** rollout of the PropertyManager.

Note: All the sheet metal parameters such as material thickness, bend radius, bend allowance, and relief that are specified while creating a base flange in the **Base Flange PropertyManager** will be used as default parameters for creating all the remaining flanges or features of the sheet metal component.

After specifying all the sheet metal parameters, click on the green tick-mark button in the **Base Flange** **PropertyManager**. A base flange of specified parameters is created, see Figure 46. Also, the **Sheet-Metal**, **Base-Flange1**, and **Flat-Pattern** nodes gets added in the FeatureManager Design Tree, see Figure 47.

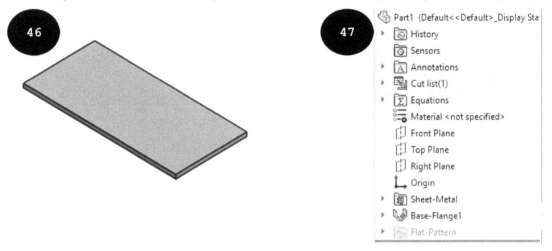

Understanding Nodes of FeatureManager Design Tree

Different nodes added to the FeatureManager Design Tree after creating a base flange are discussed next.

Sheet-Metal Node

The **Sheet-Metal** node contains all the default sheet metal parameters such as material thickness, bend radius, bend allowance, and relief that are specified while creating the base flange. These parameters get automatically assigned to all the remaining flanges or features of the sheet metal component as default parameters. However, you can edit these default parameters of a sheet metal component at any stage of the design. To do so, click on the **Sheet-Metal** node in the FeatureManager Design Tree and then click on the **Edit Feature** tool in the Pop-up toolbar that appears, see Figure 48. The **Sheet-Metal** **PropertyManager** appears. In this PropertyManager, you can edit or modify the default sheet metal parameters, as required and then exit the PropertyManager by clicking on its green tick-mark button.

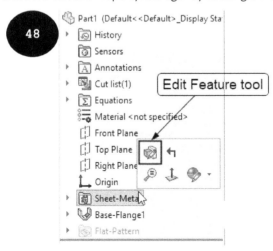

Base-Flange1 Node

The **Base-Flange1** node represents the base feature of the sheet metal component and gets added in the FeatureManager Design Tree after creating the base flange. It is used for editing or overriding the default parameters of the base flange as well as editing its sketch. To override the default parameters of the base flange, click on the **Base-Flange1** node in the FeatureManager Design Tree and then click on the **Edit Feature** tool in the Pop-up toolbar that appears, see Figure 49. The **Base-Flange1 PropertyManager** appears. In this PropertyManager, select the **Override default parameters** check box and then override the default parameters of the base flange by entering new values in the respective fields that are enabled in the PropertyManager. After overriding the default parameters, exit the PropertyManager by clicking on the green tick-mark button.

Similarly, to edit the sketch of the base flange, click on the **Base-Flange1** node and then click on the **Edit Sketch** tool in the Pop-up toolbar that appears, see Figure 50. The Sketching environment gets invoked. Now, you can edit the sketch of the base flange by using the sketching tools, as required in the Sketching environment.

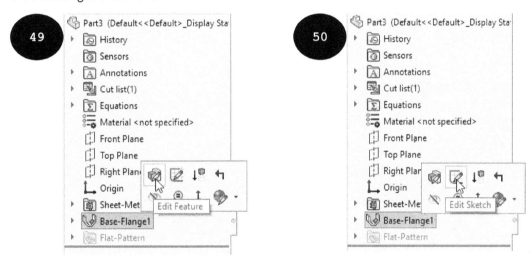

Flat-Pattern Node

The **Flat-Pattern** node is used for creating the flat pattern of the sheet metal component. By default, this node is in suppressed mode and appears in light grey color in the FeatureManager Design Tree. You will learn more about creating flat pattern of a sheet metal component later.

Creating an Edge Flange

A flange that is created on an edge of an existing flange of a sheet metal component is known as the edge flange. To create an edge flange, click on the **Edge Flange** tool in the **Sheet Metal CommandManager**, see Figure 51. The **Edge-Flange1 PropertyManager** appears, see Figure 52. Also, you are prompted to selected an edge of a planar face for creating an edge flange, since the **Edge** field is activated in the PropertyManager, by default. The options in the PropertyManager are discussed next.

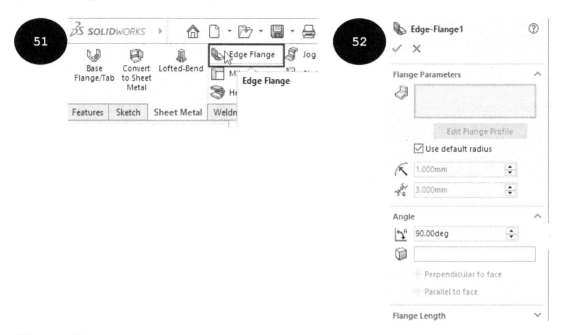

Flange Parameters

The options in the **Flange Parameters** rollout are used for selecting an edge for creating an edge flange and defining its parameters. The options are discussed next.

Edge

By default, the **Edge** field is activated in the **Flange Parameters** rollout. As a result, you can select an edge of the existing flange or feature in the graphics area. After selecting an edge, the preview of an edge flange appears along its entire length in the graphics area with two arrows, see Figure 53. Also, the name of the selected edge appears in the **Edge** field of the **Flange Parameters** rollout. Next, move the cursor to either side of the selected edge to define the direction of flange creation and then click to define the length of the edge flange arbitrarily in the graphics area. Note that as you move the cursor, the length of the flange gets increased or decreased, dynamically in the graphics area.

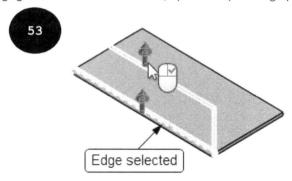

Edge selected

Note:	After defining the length of the edge flange by clicking the left mouse button, you can select other edges of existing flanges as well for creating multiple edge flanges along the selected edges.

Edit Flange Profile

The **Edit Flange Profile** button in the **Flange Parameters** rollout is used for editing the profile of the edge flange. By default, the edge flange is created along the entire length of the selected edge, refer to Figure 53. To edit the profile of the edge flange, click on the **Edit Flange Profile** button. The Sketching environment gets invoked. Also, the **Profile Sketch** dialog box appears, informing the sketch is valid, see Figure 54. Now, you can edit the sketch of the profile by using the sketching tools in the Sketching environment, as required. You can also drag the entities of the sketch to edit the width of the flange along the selected edge or the length of the flange. After editing the sketch, ensure that the sketch of the profile is valid and the message for the same appears in the **Profile Sketch** dialog box. Next, click on the **Back** button in the **Profile Sketch** dialog box for switching back to the **Edge Flange PropertyManager** for defining the remaining parameters of the edge flange. Note that if you click on the **Finish** button in this dialog box, then the edge flange of modified profile and specified parameters gets created on the selected edge. Figure 55 shows the preview of an edge flange after modifying its width along the selected edge.

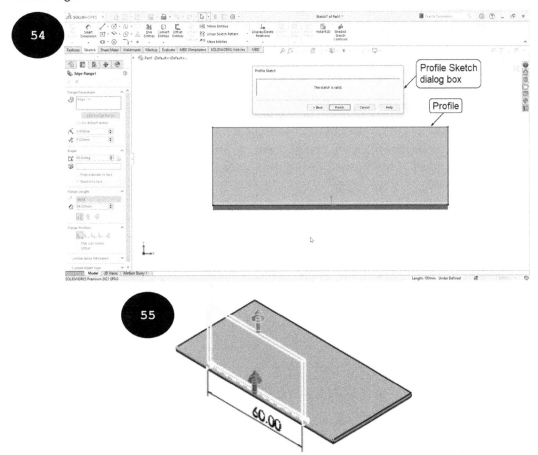

Use default radius

By default, the **Use default radius** check box is selected in the **Flange Parameters** rollout. As a result, the default bend radius is used for creating the edge flange. However, you can edit or override the default bend radius. To do so, clear the **Use default radius** check box and then enter a new bend radius value in the **Bend Radius** field that is enabled in the **Flange Parameters** rollout.

Use gauge table

The **Use gauge table** check box is used for selecting a new bend radius from the list of available bend radii in the selected gauge table. Note that this check box is enabled only if a gauge table is selected for defining the sheet metal parameters while creating the base flange of the component.

Angle

The options in the **Angle** rollout are used for defining the angle of the edge flange, see Figure 56. The options are discussed next.

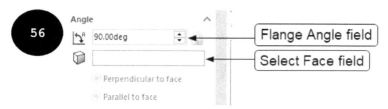

Flange Angle

By default, **90** degrees is entered in the **Flange Angle** field of the **Angle** rollout. As a result, the edge flange is created at 90 degrees angle, by default. You can enter the required angle value in this field for creating the edge flange.

Select Face

The **Select Face** field is used for creating an edge flange, perpendicular or parallel to a selected face. To do so, click on the **Select Face** field and then select a face in the graphics area. The **Perpendicular to face** and **Parallel to face** radio buttons get enabled in the rollout. Select the required radio button for creating the edge flange perpendicular or parallel to the selected face of the component, respectively.

Flange Length

The options in the **Flange Length** rollout are used for defining the length of the edge flange, see Figure 57. The options are discussed next.

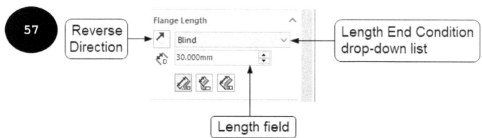

Length End Condition Drop-down List

By default, the **Blind** option is selected in the **Length End Condition** drop-down list of the **Flange Length** rollout, refer to Figure 57. As a result, you can enter the length of the edge flange in the **Length** field of the **Flange Length** rollout. You can also click on the Direction arrow that appears in the graphics area and then move the cursor upward or downward to define the length of the flange, dynamically, see Figure 58. The **Up To Vertex** option of the **Length End Condition** drop-down list is used for defining the length of the edge flange up to a selected vertex. The **Up To Edge And Merge** option is used for defining the length of the edge flange up to an edge of another body and merges the bodies together. This option is used for multi-body parts.

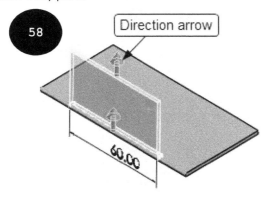

Reverse Direction

The **Reverse Direction** button in the **Flange Length** rollout is used to flip the direction of an edge flange to the other side of the selected edge. You can also click on the Reverse Direction arrow that appears in the graphics area to flip the direction of edge flange in the graphics area, see Figure 59.

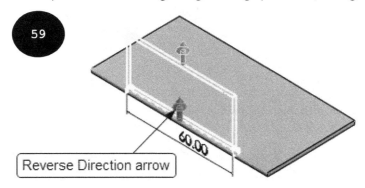

Outer Virtual Sharp

The **Outer Virtual Sharp** button in the **Flange Length** rollout is used for measuring the length of the flange from the outer virtual sharp, refer to Figure 60. The outer virtual sharp is a virtual point that is created at the intersection of edges that are tangent to the outer bend radius.

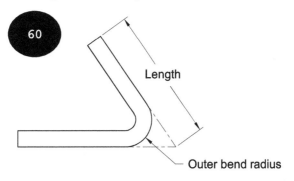

Inner Virtual Sharp

The **Inner Virtual Sharp** button is used for measuring the length of the flange from the inner virtual sharp, refer to Figure 61. The inner virtual sharp is a virtual point that is created at the intersection of edges that are tangent to the inner bend radius.

Tangent Bend

The **Tangent Bend** button is used for measuring the length of the flange from an imaginary line that is tangent to the outer bend radius and parallel to the end edge of the flange being created, refer to Figure 62. Note that this button is enabled when the bend angle is greater than 90 degrees and less than 180 degrees.

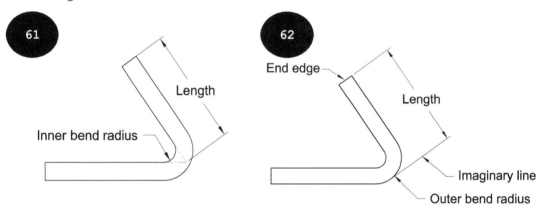

Flange Position

The options in the **Flange Position** rollout are used for defining the position of the edge flange, see Figure 63. The options are discussed next.

Material Inside

The **Material Inside** button is used for adding the flange thickness inside the maximum limit of sheet, see Figure 64.

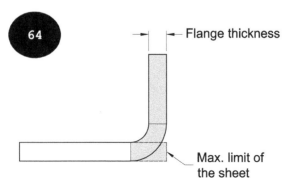

Material Outside

The **Material Outside** button is used for adding the flange thickness outside the maximum limit of sheet, see Figure 65.

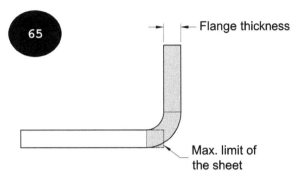

Bend Outside

The **Bend Outside** button is used for creating an edge flange such that its bend starts from the end of the maximum limit of the sheet, see Figure 66.

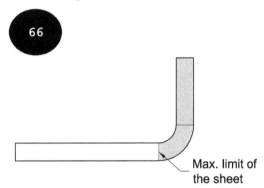

Bend from Virtual Sharp

The **Bend from Virtual Sharp** button is used for creating an edge flange such that the bending (bend angle) starts from the virtual sharp, see Figures 67 and 68. Note that the virtual sharp can either be the outer virtual sharp or the inner virtual sharp depending upon whether the **Outer Virtual Sharp** or the **Inner Virtual Sharp** button is activated in the **Flange Length** rollout of the PropertyManager.

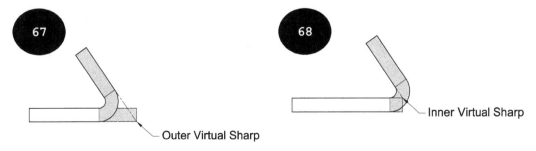

Tangent to Bend

The **Tangent to Bend** button is used for creating an edge flange such that the bend of the flange lies tangent to the maximum limit of sheet, see Figure 69. Note that this button is enabled when the bend angle is greater than 90 degrees and less than 180 degrees.

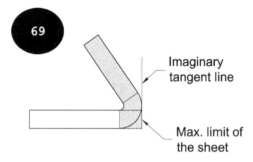

Trim side bends

The **Trim side bends** check box in the **Flange Position** rollout is used for trimming or removing the extra material in the bends of the existing side flanges, see Figures 70 and 71. In Figure 70, an edge flange is created by selecting the **Trim side bends** check box, whereas in Figure 71, an edge flange is created by clearing the **Trim side bends** check box.

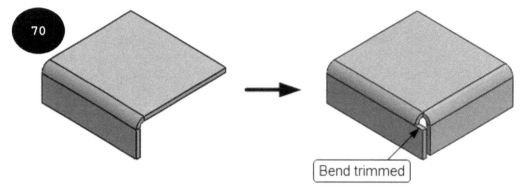

Trim side bends check box is selected

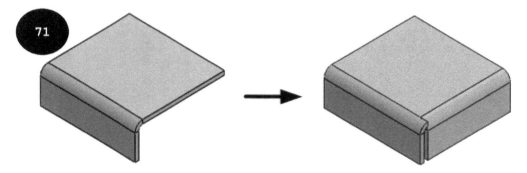

Trim side bends check box is cleared

Tip: In Figures 70 and 71, the edge flange is created by defining its position (flange thickness) inside the maximum limit of the sheet.

Offset

The **Offset** check box is used for creating an edge flange at an offset distance from the selected edge, see Figure 72. When this check box is selected, the **Offset End Condition** drop-down list and the **Offset Distance** field become available in the **Flange Position** rollout. By default, the **Blind** option is selected in the **Offset End Condition** drop-down list. As a result, you can specify an offset distance in the **Offset Distance** field of the rollout for creating an edge flange. You can also select the **Up To Vertex**, **Up To Surface**, or **Offset From Surface** option in this drop-down list for defining the end condition of an edge flange, respectively.

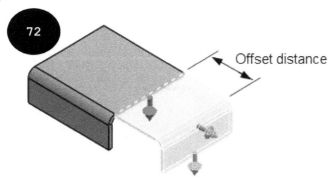

Note: The **Offset** check box is not available when the **Bend from Virtual Sharp** button is selected for defining the position of the edge flange in the **Flange Position** rollout.

Custom Bend Allowance

The options in the **Flange Position** rollout are used for customizing or overriding the default bend allowance that is defined while creating the base flange. By default, this rollout is collapsed and its options are not enabled. To enable the options of this rollout, select the check box available in its title bar. Figure 73 shows the expanded **Custom Bend Allowance** rollout. The options in this rollout are same as discussed earlier.

Custom Relief Type

The options in the **Custom Relief Type** rollout are used for customizing or overriding the default relief type that is defined while creating the base flange. By default, this rollout is collapsed and its options are not enabled. To enable the options of this rollout, select the check box available in its title bar. Figure 74 shows the expanded **Custom Relief Type** rollout. The options in this rollout are same as discussed earlier.

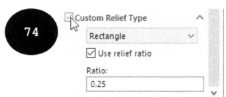

After defining all the required options for creating an edge flange, click on the green tick-mark button in the **Edge Flange PropertyManager**. An edge flange with specified parameters gets created in the graphics area.

Creating a Tab Feature

A tab feature is created by adding material equivalent to the thickness of the sheet metal component. The thickness of a tab feature is defined automatically equivalent to the thickness of the sheet and its profile or outline is defined by a sketch geometry, see Figure 75. The method for creating a tab feature is discussed below:

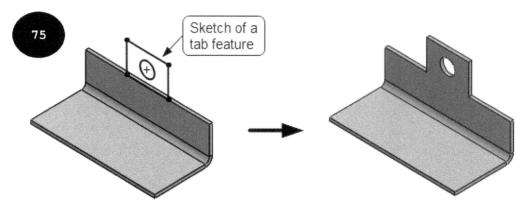

1. Click on the **Base Flange/Tab** tool in the **Sheet Metal CommandManager**, see Figure 76. The **Message PropertyManager** appears and you are prompted to either select a plane or a planar face for creating a sketch of the tab feature or an existing sketch.

2. Click on an existing face of the sheet metal component for creating the sketch of the tab feature. The Sketching environment gets invoked and the selected face gets oriented normal to the viewing direction.

Tip: If the sketch is already created in the graphics area, then you can select it as the sketch of the tab feature before or after invoking the **Base Flange/Tab** tool.

As the name of the **Base Flange/Tab** tool suggests, it is used for creating a base feature as well as a tab feature of a sheet metal component.

---

3. Create a sketch of the tab feature in the graphics area by using the sketching tools, refer to Figure 77.

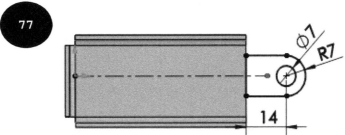

Note: The sketch of a tab feature should be a closed sketch. If you create an open sketch, the base flange will be created as a new sheet body.

4. After creating the sketch, exit the Sketching environment by clicking on the **Exit Sketch** tool in the **Sketch CommandManager**. The **Base Flange PropertyManager** appears, see Figure 78. Also, a preview of the tab feature appears in the graphics area having the same thickness as the thickness of the sheet.

Note: By default, the direction of the tab feature is defined automatically to make it coincident with the thickness of the sheet for preventing any disjoint in the component. However, if needed, you can reverse its direction to the other side of the sketching plane by selecting the **Reverse direction** check box in the PropertyManager.

Also, the **Merge result** check box is selected in the PropertyManager, by default. As a result, the resultant tab feature gets merged with the sheet. If you clear this check box, the tab feature does not merge with the sheet and creates a separate body.

5. Accept the default options and then click on the green tick-mark in the PropertyManager. The tab feature gets created, refer to Figure 79.

Creating a Miter Flange

A miter flange is a series of flanges created along the existing edges of the sheet metal component. Note that the profile or outline of a miter flange is defined by a sketch geometry that is created on a sketching plane normal to the direction of its extrusion, see Figure 80. The method for creating a miter flange is discussed below:

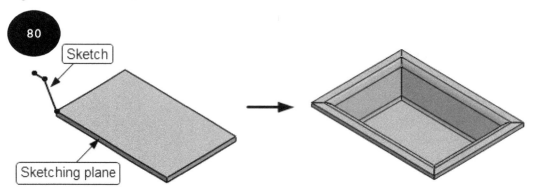

1.   Click on the **Miter Flange** tool in the **Sheet Metal CommandManager**, see Figure 81. The **Message PropertyManager** appears and you are prompted to either select a plane or a planar face for creating a sketch of a miter flange or an existing sketch.

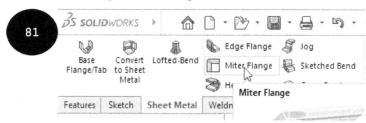

2.   Click on a planar face of the sheet metal component that is normal to the direction of extrusion of the miter flange. The Sketching environment gets invoked and the selected planar face gets oriented normal to the viewing direction.

Tip: If the sketch is already created in the graphics area, then you can select it as the sketch of the miter flange before or after invoking the **Miter Flange** tool.

3.   Create a sketch of the miter flange by using the sketching tools, refer to Figure 82.

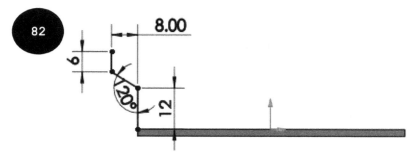

Note: The sketch of a tab feature should be a valid open sketch.

4. After creating the sketch, exit the Sketching environment by clicking on the **Exit Sketch** tool in the **Sketch CommandManager**. The **Miter Flange PropertyManager** appears, see Figure 83. Also, a preview of the miter flange appears in the graphics area along an edge normal to the sketching plane of the sheet, see Figure 84. In this figure, the orientation of the model is changed to isometric.

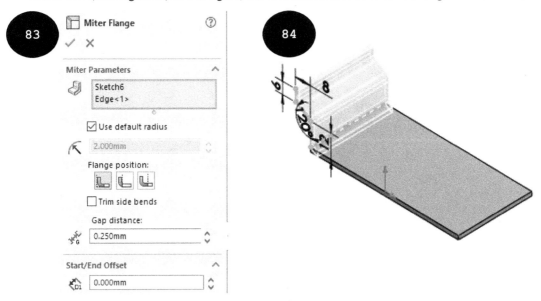

Note: By default, the **Use default radius** check box is selected in the **Miter Flange PropertyManager**. As a result, the default bend radius is used for the miter flange. However, you can override the default bend radius value by clearing the **Use default radius** check box and then entering a new bend radius in the **Bend Radius** field that is enabled below this check box in the PropertyManager.

5. Click to select other connected edges of the sheet one by one for creating a series of flanges. The preview appears along all the selected edges of the sheet, see Figure 85. Also, the names of all the selected edges appear in the **Along Edges** field of the **Miter Parameters** rollout.

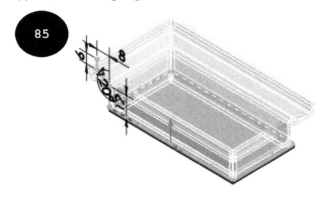

6.   Define the position of the flanges by activating the required button (**Material Inside, Material Outside,** or **Bend Outside**) in the **Flange position** area of the **Miter Parameters** rollout.

Note: The options including the **Trim side bends** check box in the **Flange position** area of the **Miter Parameters** rollout are the same as discussed earlier while creating an edge flange.

7.   Enter the required rip gap distance between the two consecutive flanges in the **Gap distance** field of the **Miter Parameters** rollout, refer to Figure 86.

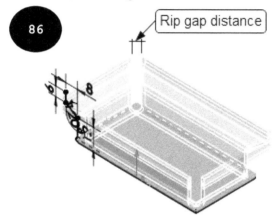

Start Offset Distance: The Start Offset Distance field in the **Start/End Offset** rollout is used for defining a start offset distance value from the start face of the miter flange, refer to Figure 87.

End Offset Distance: The End Offset Distance field in the **Start/End Offset** rollout is used for defining an end offset distance value from the end face of the miter flange, refer to Figure 88.

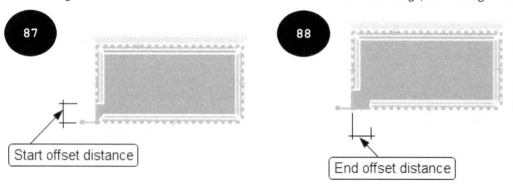

Note: The start offset distance is applied to the first selected edge, whereas the end offset distance is applied to the last selected edge of a series of continuous flanges.

By default, 0 (zero) is entered in the **Start Offset Distance** and **End Offset Distance** fields. As a result, the flanges on the first and last selected edges are created along their full length without any offset distance.

8. If needed, enter the required start and end offset distance values in the **Start Offset Distance** and the **End Offset Distance** fields of the **Start/End Offset** rollout, respectively.

Note: The options in the **Custom Bend Allowance** and **Custom Relief Type** rollouts of the PropertyManager are used for customizing or overriding the default bend allowance and relief type that are defined while creating the base flange. The options are same as discussed earlier.

---

9. Click on the green tick-mark button in the PropertyManager. The miter flange is created on the selected edges of the sheet, see Figure 89.

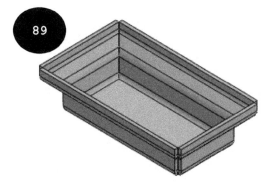

Creating a Sketched Bend

A sketched bend is a bend created by using a sketch line as the bending line, see Figure 90. The method for creating a sketched bend is discussed below:

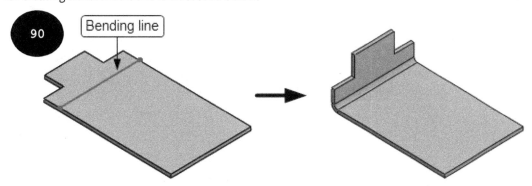

1. Invoke the Sketching environment by selecting a planar face of the sheet on which a bending line is to be created.

2. Create a line as the bending line by using the **Line** tool, refer to Figure 91.

Tip: The bending line does not necessarily need to be created through the entire length of the sheet. Also, you can create it before or after invoking the **Sketched Bend** tool.

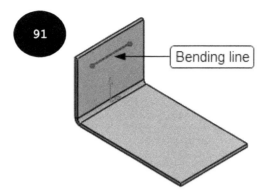

3. After creating a bending line, click on the **Sheet Metal** tab in the CommandManager and then click on the **Sketched Bend** tool, see Figure 92. The **Sketched Bend PropertyManager** appears, see Figure 93. Also, you are prompted to specify the planar face to be fixed when creating the bend, since the **Fixed Face** field is activated in the PropertyManager, by default.

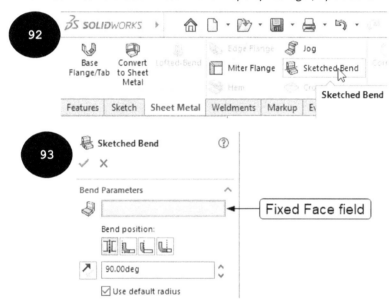

4. Click to define the fixed face (a side of the bending line) of the sheet that will be fixed after creating the bend, refer to Figure 94. The preview of a sketched bend appears, see Figure 95.

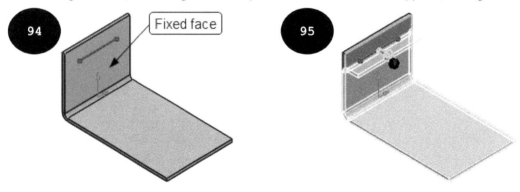

5. Define the position of the bend by activating the required button (**Bend Centerline, Material Inside, Material Outside,** or **Bend Outside**) in the **Bend position** area of the **Bend Parameters** rollout.

Note: By default, the **Bend Centerline** button is activated in the **Bend position** area of the **Bend Parameters** rollout. As a result, the sheet thickness is added equally on both the sides of the bending line. The remaining options in this area are the same as discussed earlier.

6. Enter the bend angle in the **Bend Angle** field of the **Bend Parameters** rollout, as required.

7. Click on the **Reverse Direction** button in the **Bend Parameters** rollout of the PropertyManager to flip the bend direction on the other side of the sheet.

Note: By default, the **Use default radius** check box is selected in the **Sketched Bend PropertyManager**. As a result, the default bend radius is used for the sketched bend. However, you can override the default bend radius value by clearing the **Use default radius** check box and then entering a new bend radius in the **Bend Radius** field that is enabled below this check box in the PropertyManager.

8. Click on the green tick-mark button in the PropertyManager. A sketched bend is created, see Figure 96.

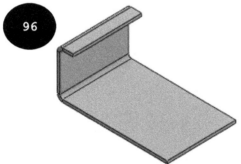

96

Note: You can also create multiple sketched bends by using a single sketch. To do so, create more than one sketch line as the bending lines on the selected planar face, refer to Figure 97. This figure shows two bending lines created as a single sketch, a fixed face, and the resultant sketched bends.

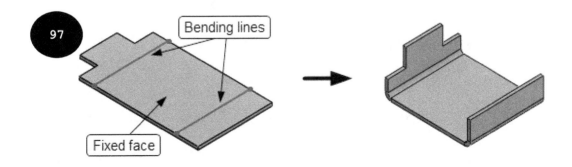

97

Bending lines

Fixed face

Creating a Jog Bend

A jog bend consists of two bends created by using a single bending line, see Figure 98. The method for creating a sketched bend is discussed below:

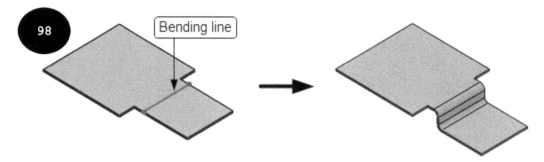

1. Invoke the Sketching environment by selecting a planar face of the sheet on which a bending line is to be created.

2. Create a line as the bending line by using the **Line** tool, refer to Figure 99.

Note: The sketch of the jog bend must contains a single line. Also, it is not necessary to be created through the entire length of the face, refer to Figure 99. Moreover, it is not necessary to be horizontal or vertical.

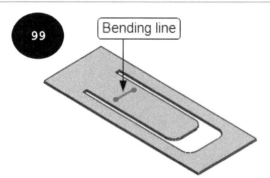

3. After creating a bending line, click on the **Sheet Metal** tab in the CommandManager and then click on the **Jog** tool, see Figure 100. The **Jog PropertyManager** appears, see Figure 101. Also, you are prompted to specify the planar face to be fixed when creating the jog bend, since the **Fixed Face** field is activated in the PropertyManager, by default.

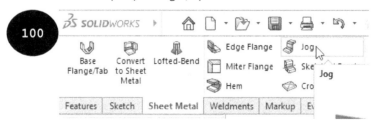

Tip: You can create the bending line before and after invoking the **Jog** tool.

4. Click to define the fixed face of the sheet that will be fixed after creating the jog bend. The preview of a jog bend which consists of two bends appears in the graphics area, see Figure 102.

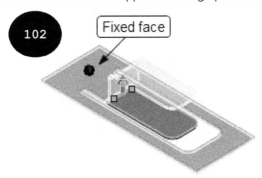

Note: By default, the **Use default radius** check box is selected in the **Jog PropertyManager**. As a result, the default bend radius is used for the bends. However, you can override the default bend radius value by clearing the **Use default radius** check box and then entering a new bend radius in the **Bend Radius** field that is enabled below this check box in the PropertyManager.

5. Ensure that the **Blind** option is selected in the **End Condition** drop-down list of the **Jog Offset** rollout for defining the termination of the jog offset by entering an offset distance value.

Note: You can also select the **Up To Vertex**, **Up To Surface**, or **Offset From Surface** option in the **End Condition** drop-down list for defining the jog offset, respectively.

6. Enter the required jog offset distance value in the **Offset Distance** field, refer to Figure 103.

Note: The jog offset distance is measured depending upon the button (**Outside Offset, Inside Offset,** or **Overall Dimension**) activated in the **Dimension position** area of the **Jog Offset** rollout, see Figure 104.

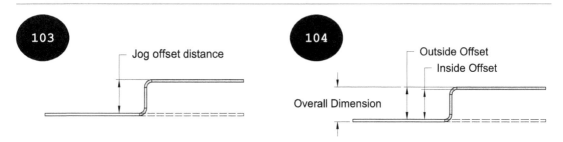

7. Click to activate the required button (**Outside Offset, Inside Offset,** or **Overall Dimension**) in the **Dimension position** area of the **Jog Offset** rollout for measuring the jog offset dimension, as required, refer to Figure 104.

    Fix projected length: By default, the **Fix projected length** check box is selected in the **Jog Offset** rollout. As a result, the length of the bent sheet after jog bend is maintained equal to the projected length of the sheet, see Figure 105. If you clear this check box, the length of the bent sheet is maintained equal to the original length of the sheet, see Figure 106.

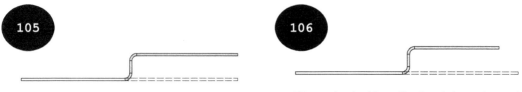

Fix projected length check box selected   Fix projected length check box cleared

8. Select or clear the **Fix projected length** check box in the **Offset** rollout, as required.

9. Define the position of the bends by activating the required button (**Bend Centerline, Material Inside, Material Outside,** or **Bend Outside**) in the **Jog Position** rollout. All these buttons are same as discussed earlier.

10. Enter the required angle of the jog bend in the **Jog Angle** field of the **Jog Angle** rollout, see Figures 107 and 108. In Figure 107, the jog angle is defined as 90 degrees, whereas and in Figure 108, the jog angle is defined as 135 degrees.

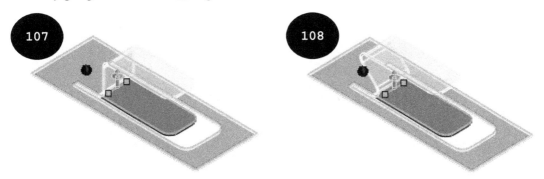

11. Click on the green tick-mark button in the PropertyManager. The jog bend of specified parameters is created, see Figure 109.

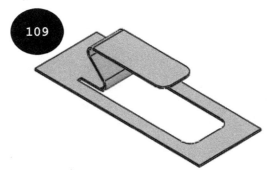

Creating a Hem Feature

A hem feature is created by curling a sheet in order to remove its sharp edges that may cause injury while handling the component, see Figure 110. The method for creating a hem feature is discussed below:

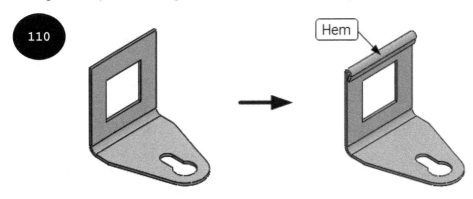

1. Click on the **Hem** tool in the **Sheet Metal CommandManager**, see Figure 111. The **Hem PropertyManager** appears, see Figure 112.

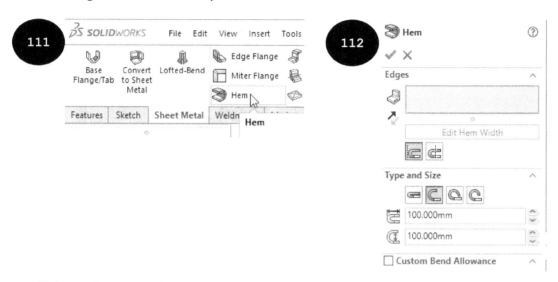

2.   Click to select edges of the sheet metal component for creating a hem feature, see Figure 113. The preview appears such that the selected edges get curled as per the default parameters, see Figure 114.

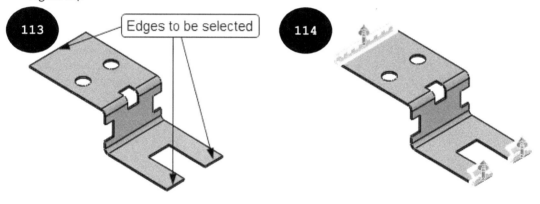

Edges to be selected

Note: The selected edge for creating a hem must be a linear edge.

Edit Hem Width: The Edit Hem Width button is used for editing the width of a hem profile along a selected edge. To do so, select an edge in the **Edges** field of the PropertyManager for editing the width of its hem profile and then click on the **Edit Hem Width** button. The Sketching environment gets invoked. Also, the **Profile Sketch** dialog box appears, informing that the sketch is valid. Now, you can drag the hem profile (sketch entity) along the selected edge for editing its width, as required. You can also use the sketching tools for editing the width of the hem profile along the selected edge. After editing the width of the hem profile, ensure that it is valid and the message for the same appears in the **Profile Sketch** dialog box. Next, click on the **Back** button in the **Profile Sketch** dialog box for switching back to the **Hem PropertyManager** for defining the remaining parameters of the hem feature. Note that if you click on the **Finish** button in the **Profile Sketch** dialog box, then the hem feature with specified parameters gets created on the selected edge or edges. Figure 115 shows the preview of a hem feature after editing the width of a hem profile along an edge.

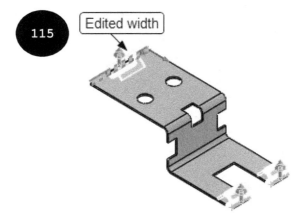

3. Edit the width of the hem profile for one or more selected edges one by one by using the **Edit Hem Width** button, if needed.

4. Click on the required button (**Material Inside** or **Material Outside**) in the **Edges** rollout of the PropertyManager for defining the material thickness inside or outside the maximum limit of the sheet, as required.

5. Click on the **Reverse Direction** button in the **Edges** rollout of the PropertyManager to reverse the direction of hem, if needed.

6. Select the required type of hem to be created by clicking on the required button (**Closed, Open, Tear Drop,** or **Rolled**) in the **Type and Size** rollout of the PropertyManager, see Figure 116.

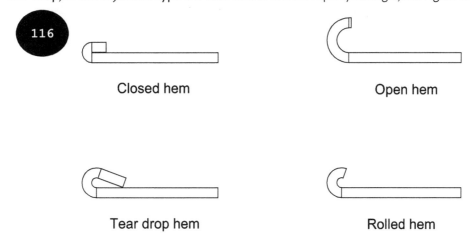

7. Define the hem parameters such as length, angle, and radius in the respective fields of the **Type and Size** rollout. Note that the availability of fields in this rollout for defining the hem parameters depend upon the type of hem selected.

Note: You can also customize or override the bend allowance and relief type by using the **Custom Bend Allowance** and **Custom Relief Type** rollout of the PropertyManager, as discussed earlier.

8.   Click on the green tick-mark button in the PropertyManager. The hem feature with specified parameters is created, see Figure 117.

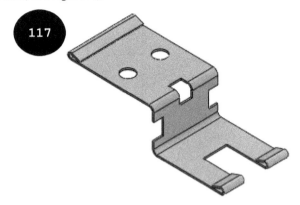

Closing Corners

A closed corner is created by filling the gap between adjacent flanges of a sheet metal component, see Figure 118. The method for creating a closed corner is discussed below:

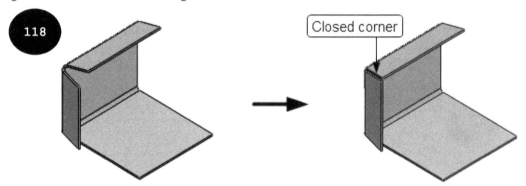

1.   Click on **Corners > Closed Corner** in the **Sheet Metal CommandManager**, see Figure 119. The **Closed Corner PropertyManager** appears, see Figure 120. Also, you are prompted to select planar corner face(s) to extend for creating a closed corner, since the **Faces to Extend** field is activated in the PropertyManager, by default.

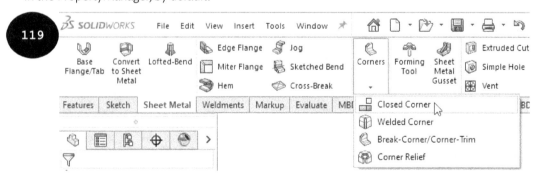

2. Select a planar face of a corner as the face to be extended, see Figure 121. The preview of a closed corner appears in the graphics area, since SOLIDWORKS automatically attempts to find the face to match with it for creating a closed corner, since the **Auto propagation** check box is selected in the PropertyManager, by default, see Figure 122. Note that the name of the matched face or faces displayed in the **Faces to Match** field of the PropertyManager.

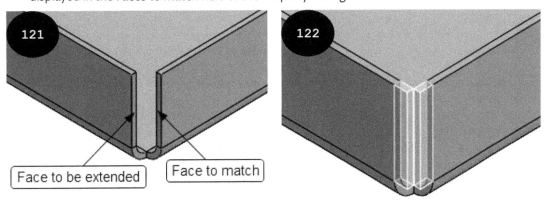

Note: You can select one or more planar faces to be extended one after another for creating multiple closed corners in the **Faces to Extend** field of the PropertyManager.

If SOLIDWORKS is unable to find matching faces automatically, then you need to manually select them by using the **Faces to Match** field of the PropertyManager.

3. Define the corner type to be created by activating the required button (**Butt, Overlap,** or **Underlap**) in the **Corner type** area of the PropertyManager, see Figure 123.

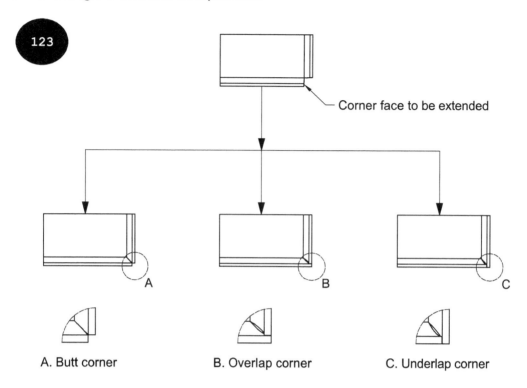

A. Butt corner   B. Overlap corner   C. Underlap corner

4.   Enter the required gap distance between the two faces (extended face and matched face) of the closed corner in the **Gap distance** field of the PropertyManager.

5.   Enter the overlap/underlap ratio between the material that overlaps and the material that underlaps while creating a closed corner in the **Overlap/underlap ratio** field of the PropertyManager. Note that this field is enabled only when the **Overlap** or **Underlap** button is activated in the **Corner type** area of the PropertyManager. Also, the ratio 1 indicates that the overlap and the underlap material is equivalent.

Open bend region: On selecting the **Open bend region** check box, the closed corner is created such that its bend region remains open, see Figures 124 and 125.

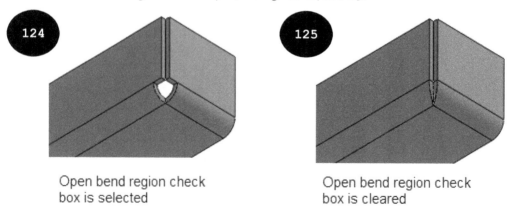

Open bend region check
box is selected

Open bend region check
box is cleared

Coplanar faces: On selecting the **Coplanar faces** check box, the closed corner is created such that all the faces that are coplanar to the selected extended face get selected for creating the closed corner, see Figures 126 and 127.

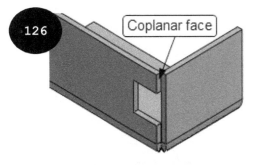

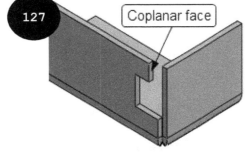

Coplanar faces check box is selected

Coplanar faces check box is cleared

Narrow corner: On selecting the **Narrow corner** check box, the closed corner is created such that its bend area gets narrow by using an algorithm in the large bend radii, see Figures 128 and 129.

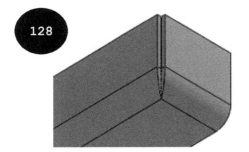

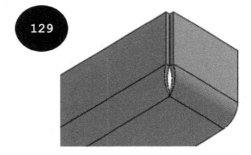

Narrow corner check box is selected

Narrow corner check box is cleared

Auto propagation: By default, the **Auto propagation** check box is selected. As a result, the faces to be matched get selected automatically on selecting the faces to be extended for creating closed corners.

6.   Select or clear the **Open bend region**, **Coplanar faces**, **Narrow corner**, and **Auto propagation** check boxes in the PropertyManager, as required.

7.   Click on the green tick-mark button in the PropertyManager. A closed corner is created between the selected faces of the sheet metal component.

Welding Corners

A welded corner is created by adding a weld bead at the corner of a sheet metal component, see Figure 130. The method for creating a welded corner is discussed below:

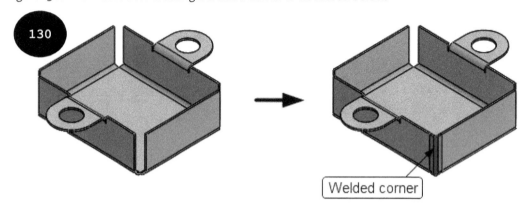

Welded corner

Note: A welded corner can be created between two flanges which includes miter flanges, edge flanges, and closed corner flanges.

---

1. Click on **Corners > Welded Corner** in the **Sheet Metal CommandManager**, see Figure 131. The **Welded Corner PropertyManager** appears, see Figure 132. Also, you are prompted to select a face (side face) of the corner to be welded, since the **Select a side face of a sheet metal corner to be welded** field is activated in the PropertyManager, by default.

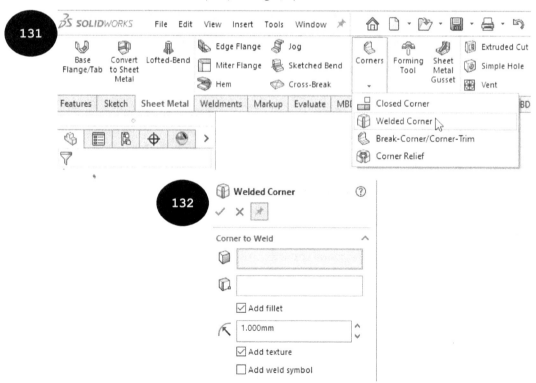

2. Select a face (side face) of the corner to be welded in the graphics area, see Figure 133. The preview of a welded corner appears in the graphics area, see Figure 134. Also, the name of the selected face displayed in the **Select a side face of a sheet metal corner to be welded** field of the PropertyManager.

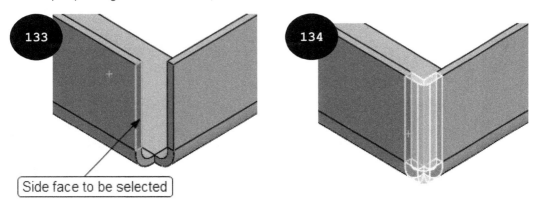

Stopping point: The Stopping point field in the PropertyManager is used for selecting a vertex, an edge, or a face to define a stopping point where the weld bead ends.

3. Click on the **Stopping point** field in the PropertyManager and then select a vertex, an edge, or a face as the stopping point for ending the weld bead, if needed.

Add fillet: On selecting the **Add fillet** check box, a fillet of specified radius value gets added in the resultant welded corner, see Figures 135 and 136.

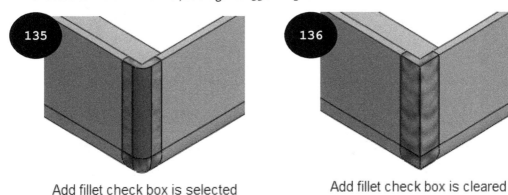

Add fillet check box is selected   Add fillet check box is cleared

4. Select or clear the **Add fillet** check box in the PropertyManager, as required.

5. Enter the required fillet radius in the **Fillet radius** field of the PropertyManager. Note that this field is enabled only when the **Add fillet** check box is selected.

6. Select the **Add texture** check box in the PropertyManager for adding a texture to the weld bead.

7. Select the **Add weld symbol** check box in the PropertyManager for adding a weld symbol.

8. Click on the green tick-mark button in the PropertyManager. A welded corner is created.

Breaking Corners

In SOLIDWORKS, you can break the corner edges of a sheet metal component by creating chamfers or fillets, see Figure 137. The method for breaking corners is discussed below:

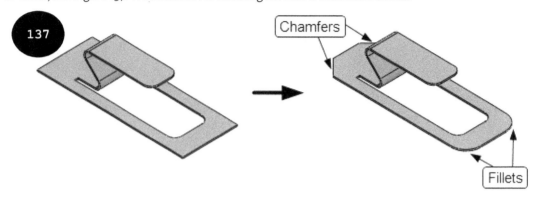

1. Click on **Corners > Break-Corner/Corner-Trim** in the **Sheet Metal CommandManager**, see Figure 138. The **Break Corner PropertyManager appears**, see Figure 139. Also, you are prompted to select corner edge(s) or flange face(s), since the **Corner Edges and/or Flange Faces** field is activated in the PropertyManager, by default.

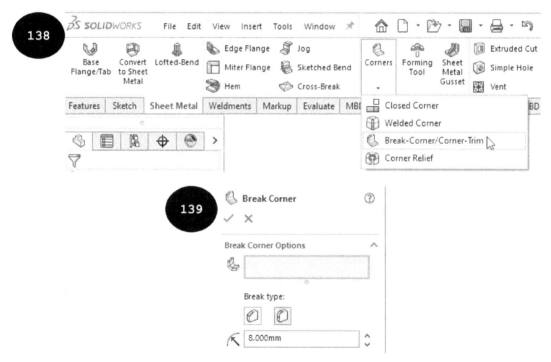

2. Select one or more corner edges or faces of a sheet metal component. The preview of chamfers or fillets appears on the selected edges depending upon whether the **Chamfer** or **Fillet** button is activated in the **Break type** area of the PropertyManager, see Figure 140.

Note: On selecting a face, all the outer edges of the selected face gets chamfered or filleted, see Figure 141.

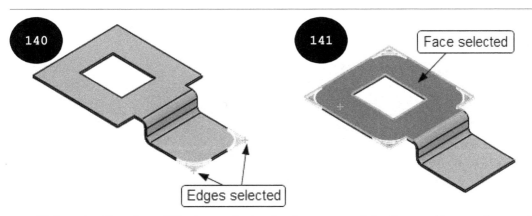

3. Click on the **Chamfer** or **Fillet** button in the **Break type** area of the PropertyManager for creating chamfers or fillets on the selected edges, respectively.

4. Enter the chamfer distance or fillet radius in the **Distance** or **Radius** field of the PropertyManager, respectively. Note that the availability of the field depends upon whether the **Chamfer** or **Fillet** button is activated in the **Break type** area of the PropertyManager.

5. Click on the green tick-mark button in the PropertyManager. The selected corner edges get broken such that the fillets or chamfers are created.

Adding Corner Reliefs

You can add corner relief treatments between 2 or 3 bend corners of a sheet metal component by using the **Corner Relief** tool. It helps to prevent the unwanted deformation in the sheet metal component while creating its flat pattern. The method for adding corner reliefs is discussed below:

1. Click on **Corners > Corner Relief** in the **Sheet Metal CommandManager**, see Figure 142. The **Corner Relief PropertyManager** appears, see Figure 143.

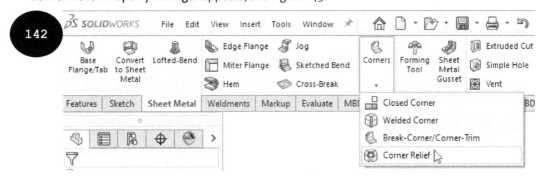

2. Select the **2 Bend Corner** or **3 Bend Corner** radio button in the **Corner Type** rollout for adding corner reliefs between 2 bend corners or 3 bend corners of the sheet, respectively.

3. Ensure that the sheet metal component (body) is selected in the field of the **Scope** rollout as the body for applying the corner reliefs.

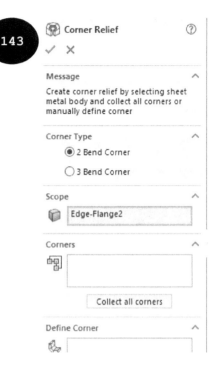

4. Click on the **Select a corner to set or change relief type** field in the **Corners** rollout to select the corners for applying the reliefs.

5. Click on the **Collect all corners** button in the **Corners** rollout of the PropertyManager. All the corners get listed in the **Select a corner to set or change relief type** field of the **Corners** rollout depending upon the whether the **2 Bend Corner** or **3 Bend Corner** radio button is selected. Also, the same gets highlighted in the graphics area, see Figure 144. In this figure, two corners (3 bend corners) get highlighted in the graphics area.

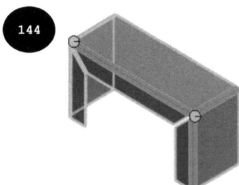

6. Select a corner from the list of corners in the **Select a corner to set or change relief type** field of the **Corners** rollout. The faces that define the selected corner are displayed in the **Define Corner** rollout of the PropertyManager.

7. Select the required relief type (**Rectangular, Circular, Tear, Full Round,** or **suitcase**) to be applied to the selected corner in the drop-down list of the **Relief Options** rollout.

8. Define the other relief parameters in the **Relief Options** rollout of the PropertyManager. Note that the availability of options in this rollout depends upon the relief type selected.

9. Similarly, define the relief type and its parameters for other corners of the sheet.

10. Click on the green tick-mark button in the PropertyManager. The corner reliefs with specified parameters get applied to the selected corners in the sheet metal component, see Figure 145. This figure shows 3 bend corners before and after applying the circular corner relief with specific parameters.

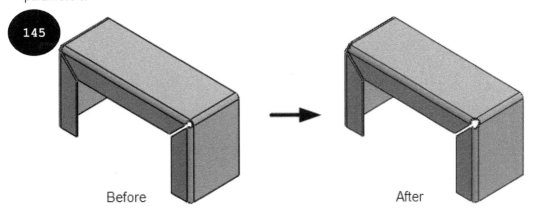

Before   After

Creating a Lofted Bend

A lofted bend is created by lofting two open sections (sketches) such that the sheet transits from one section to another, see Figure 146. This figure shows two open sections and the resultant lofted bend. The method for creating a lofted bend is discussed below:

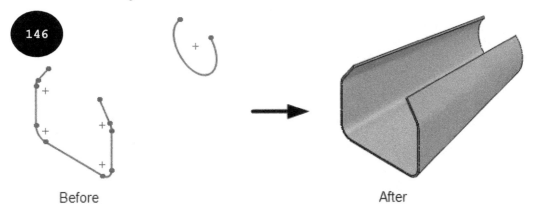

Before   After

1. Click on the **Lofted-Bend** tool in the **Sheet Metal CommandManager**, see Figure 147. The **Lofted Bends PropertyManager** appears, see Figure 148.

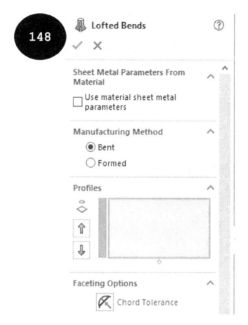

Manufacturing Method: The Bent radio button in the **Manufacturing Method** rollout is used for creating a lofted bend feature with real physical bends at the bend regions, see Figure 149. It forms a realistic transition between two sections to facilitate instruction for press brake manufacturing. The **Formed** radio button is used for creating a lofted bend feature with rolled or smooth transition at bend regions, see Figure 150.

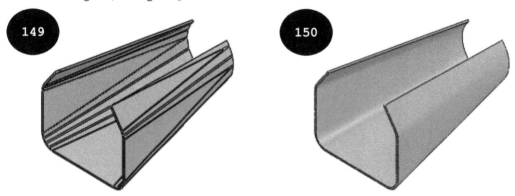

2.   Select the required radio button (**Bent** or **Formed**) in the **Manufacturing Method** rollout in the PropertyManager.

3.   Select two open sections in the **Profiles** rollout of the PropertyManager.

> **Note:** The point of selection for selecting both the sections (profiles) of the lofted bend feature should be in one direction in order to avoid twisting in the resultant feature. Also, the sections (profiles) should not have vertices for creating a formed lofted bend feature. If the sections have vertices, you can replace them with fillets.

Faceting Options: The Faceting Options rollout appears only when the **Bent** radio button is selected in the **Manufacturing Method** rollout of the PropertyManager and is used for defining the faceting option for the bends. The **Chord Tolerance** button is used for defining the maximum distance or deviation between the original sketch geometry and the facet face in a bend region, refer to Figure 151. The **Number of Bends** button is used for defining the number of bends in a bend region. The **Segment Length** button is used for defining the maximum length of the facet face (linear segment) in a bend region. The **Segment Angle** button is used for defining the maximum angle between two adjacent facet faces in a bend region.

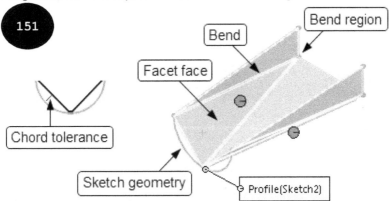

4. Click on the required button (**Chord Tolerance, Number of Bends, Segment Length**, or **Segment Angle**) in the **Faceting Options** rollout of the PropertyManager, as discussed above.

5. Depending upon the faceting option selected in the **Faceting Options** rollout, enter the facet value in the field of the **Facet Value** rollout. For example, if the **Number of Bends** button is selected in the **Faceting Options** rollout, then you can enter the number of bends to be created in a bend region as the facet value in the field of the **Facet Value** rollout.

Refer to endpoint: By default, the **Refer to endpoint** check box is selected in the **Facet Value** rollout. As a result, the lofted bend segments get translated such that a sharp corner is formed at the bend regions, see Figure 152. If this check box is cleared, the sharp corner gets replaced with adjacent bends such that an approximated arc is created at the corner, see Figure 153.

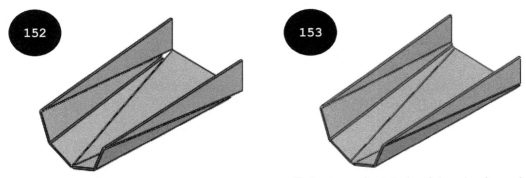

Refer to endpoint check box is selected   Refer to endpoint check box is cleared

6. Select or clear the **Refer to endpoint** check box in the **Facet Value** rollout, as discussed above.

Note: By default, the defined faceting option applies to all bend regions of the lofted bend feature. However, you can also define the faceting option individually to a bend region. To do so, click on the pink dot of a bend region in the graphics area whose faceting option is to be defined, see Figure 154. The **Faceting options** dialog box appears, see Figure 155. In this dialog box, select the required button (**Chord Tolerance, Number of Bends, Segment Length,** or **Segment Angle**) as the faceting option and then its facet value. Next, click on the green tick-mark button in the dialog box. The selected faceting option gets defined for the selected bend region. Similarly, you can define the faceting option for the other bend regions, individually.

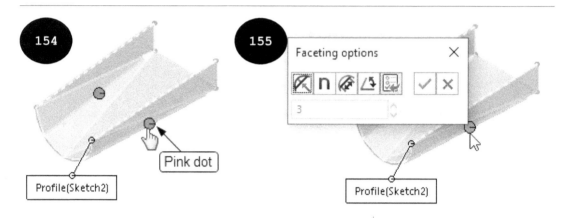

Tip: You can also customize the sheet metal parameters, bend allowance, and relief by using the options available in the **Sheet Metal Parameters, Bend Allowance,** and **Auto Relief** rollouts of the PropertyManager. The options in these rollouts are same as discussed earlier.

7. After defining all the parameters, click on the green tick-mark button in the PropertyManager. A lofted feature gets created.

Creating an Extruded Cut Feature

In SOLIDWORKS, you can create an extruded cut on a planar face of a sheet metal component. Creating extruded cuts on a sheet metal component is similar to creating cuts on a solid model. The method for creating an extruded cut feature on a sheet metal component is discussed below:

1. Click on the **Extruded Cut** tool in the **Sheet Metal CommandManager**, see Figure 156. The **Extrude PropertyManager** appears. Also, you are prompted to either select a plane or a planar face for creating a sketch of the extruded cut feature or select an existing sketch.

Tip: If the sketch is already created in the graphics area, then you can select it as the sketch of the extruded cut feature before or after invoking the **Extruded Cut** tool.

2. Select a planar face of the sheet metal component or a plane as the sketching plane. The Sketching environment gets invoked and the selected planar face gets orientated normal to the viewing direction.

3. Create a sketch of the extruded cut feature by using the sketching tools, see Figure 157.

4. After creating the sketch, exit the Sketching environment. The **Cut-Extrude PropertyManager** appears, see Figure 158. Also, a preview of the cut feature appears in the graphics area.

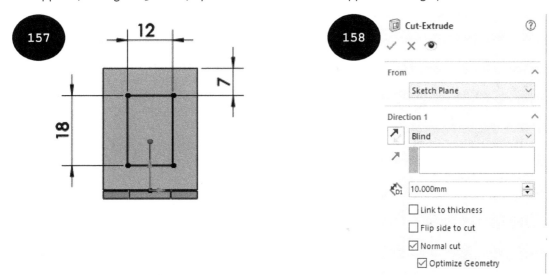

5. Define the depth of the extruded cut feature by using the required option such as **Blind, Through All, Up To Next**, or **Up To Surface** in the **End Condition** drop-down list of the PropertyManager. The options for defining the depth of the extrude cut feature on a sheet metal component are same as those defining the depth of the extrude cut feature on a solid model.

Note: You can also define the depth of the cut feature equal to the thickness of the sheet metal component by selecting the **Link to thickness** check box in the PropertyManager. This check box is available only when the **Blind** option is selected in the **End Condition** drop-down list of the PropertyManager. When the **Link to thickness** check box is selected, the depth of the extruded cut feature gets automatically adjusted or defined equal to the thickness of the sheet.

Flip side to cut: On selecting the **Flip side to cut** check box, the side of the material to be removed gets reversed.

Normal cut: On selecting the **Normal cut** check box, the resultant cut feature is created normal to the sheet metal thickness, see Figure 159. On clearing this check box, the resultant cut feature is created normal to the sketching plane, see Figure 160.

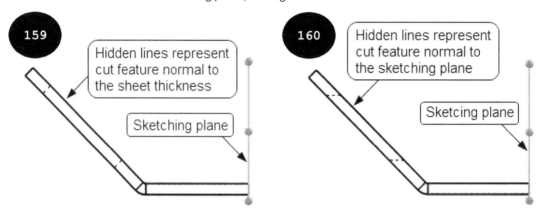

Note: Figures 159 and 160 show the side view of the sheet metal component in which a cut feature is created when the **Normal cut** check box is selected and cleared, respectively.

Optimize Geometry: On selecting the **Optimize Geometry** check box, the cut geometry gets optimized in order to avoid any irregularities or problematic shapes in the resultant cut feature when cutting through an angle or curved face.

6.   Select or clear the **Normal cut** check box in the PropertyManager, as required.

7.   Click on the green tick-mark button in the PropertyManager. An extruded cut feature is created, see Figure 161.

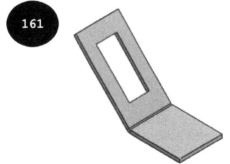

Creating a Forming Tool

A forming tool is a solid part that act as a die for creating formed features like embosses, louvers, and lances. These formed features are not straight-line bends, rather they represent the features that are created by stamping, punching, or drawn operations, refer to Figure 162. SOLIDWORKS is provided with some sample forming tool parts to get started with creating formed features on a sheet metal component. You can access these forming tool parts in the **forming tools** sub-folder of the **design library** folder in the **Design Library Task Panel**, refer to Figure 163.

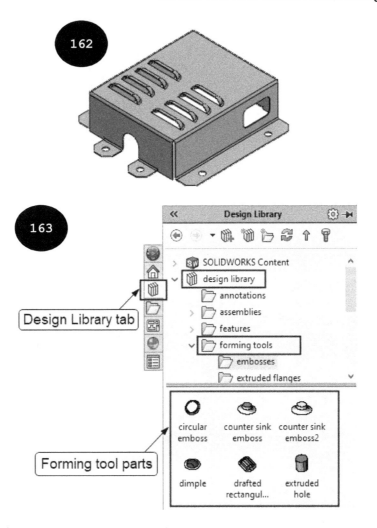

If the **Design library** folder is not available in the **Design Library Task Panel**, then you need to customize to add it. To do so, click on the **Options** tool in the **Standard** toolbar. The **System Options** dialog box appears. In this dialog box, click on the **File Locations** option in its left panel and then select the **Design Library** option in the **Show folders for** drop-down list that appears in the right panel of the dialog box, see Figure 164. Next, click on the **Add** button in the dialog box. The **Select Folder** dialog box appears. In this dialog box, browse to the location C:\ProgramData\SOLIDWORKS\SOLIDWORKS 2021 and then select the **design library** folder. Next, click on the **Select Folder** button in the dialog box. The location for **Design Library** gets defined to C:\ProgramData\SOLIDWORKS\SOLIDWORKS 2021\design library. Next, click on the OK button in the dialog box. The **SOLIDWORKS** message window appears. Click on the **Yes** button to accept the changes and display the **design library** folder in the **Design Library Task Panel**.

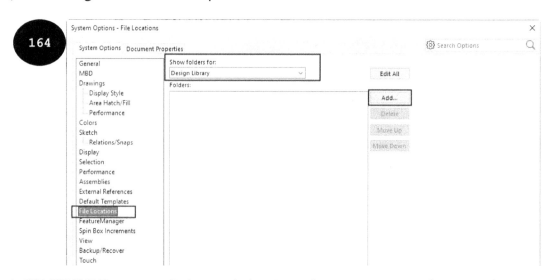

In SOLIDWORKS, you can edit the sample forming tool parts or create new forming tool parts, as required. Note that the forming tool parts can be dragged on the required faces of the sheet metal component for creating the respective formed features. However, before you learn about creating a formed feature, it is important to first learn about creating a new forming tool part and the same is discussed below:

1. Invoke the Part modeling environment and then create a solid part as the forming tool by using the features modeling tools available in the **Features CommandManager**, refer to Figures 165 and 166.

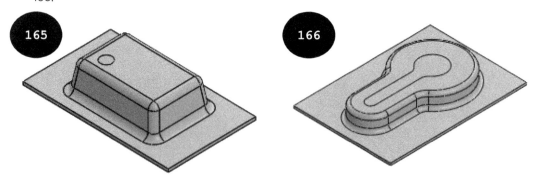

Note: To learn creating 3D solid parts, assemblies, and drawings, refer to "**SOLIDWORKS 2021: A Power Guide for Beginners and Intermediate User**" textbook by CADArtifex.

After creating a 3D solid part, you can convert it into a forming tool.

2. Click on the **Forming Tool** tool in the **Sheet Metal CommandManager** for creating a forming tool, see Figure 167. The **Form Tool PropertyManager** appears, see Figure 168. Also, you are prompted to select a stopping face, since the **Stopping Face** field is activated in the PropertyManager, by default.

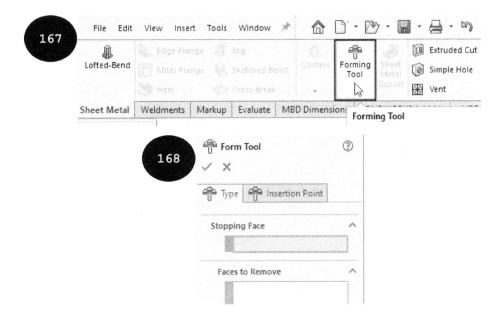

Stopping Face: The Stopping Face field is used for defining the stopping face of the forming tool where it stops when inserted on a sheet metal component, see Figures 169 and 170.

Faces to Remove: The Faces to Remove field is used for defining a face or faces of the forming tool to be removed when inserted on a sheet metal component, see Figures 169 and 170. Note that you can also create a forming tool without selecting any face to be removed. On doing so, none of the face of the forming tool gets removed in the resultant sheet metal component.

Note: You will learn about inserting a formatting tool on a sheet metal component for creating a formed feature later.

3. Click to define a stopping face of the forming tool, see Figures 169 and 170.

4. After defining the stopping face, click on the **Faces to Remove** field in the PropertyManager and then select a face or faces of the forming tool to be removed when it is inserted on a sheet metal component, see Figures 169 and 170.

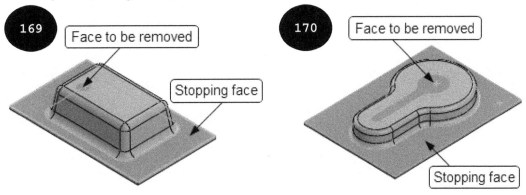

Tip: If you do not want to remove any faces of the forming tool in the resultant sheet metal component, then do not select any faces in the **Faces to Remove** field.

Insertion Point Tab: The Insertion Point tab in the **Form Tool PropertyManager** allows you to define the position of the insertion point for the forming tool part by applying dimensions and relations, as required. When you click on this tab, the insertion point for the forming tool appears at its default position on the defined stopping face. Now, you can apply dimensions or relations to define its new position on the stopping face, as required.

5. Define the position of the insertion point for the forming tool by using the **Insertion Point** tab, if needed. You can also skip this step and accept the default position of the insertion point.

6. Click on the green tick-mark button in the PropertyManager. A forming tool part gets created.

Note: In a forming tool part, the stopping face appears in cyan color and the face or faces to be removed appear in red color.

After creating a forming tool part, you need to save it as a forming tool.

7. Press the CTRL + S keys or click on the **Save** tool in the **Standard** toolbar. The **Save As** dialog box appears.

Tip: If the part file is already saved then you need to click on **File > Save As** in the SOLIDWORKS Menus to invoke the **Save As** dialog box.

8. Select the **Form Tool (*.sldftp)** as the file type in the **Save as type** drop-down list of the **Save As** dialog box. The location to save the forming tool gets browsed automatically to **design library** folder at *C:\ProgramData\SOLIDWORKS\SOLIDWORKS 2021\design library* in the dialog box.

9. Double-click on the **forming tools** folder in the **design library** folder of the **Save As** dialog box.

Note: You can save the forming tool part in the **forming tools** folder or any of its existing sub-folders. You can also create a new folder in the **forming tools** folder and then save the forming tool in it.

10. Enter a name for the forming tool part in the **File name** field of the **Save As** dialog box and then click on the **Save** button. The forming tool part gets saved at the *C:\ProgramData\SOLIDWORKS\ SOLIDWORKS 2021\design library\forming tools* location.

Inserting a Forming Tool

After creating a forming tool part and saving it at the desired location, you can insert it on the face of a sheet metal component for creating the respective formed feature, refer to Figures 171 and 172. The method for inserting a forming tool part is discussed below:

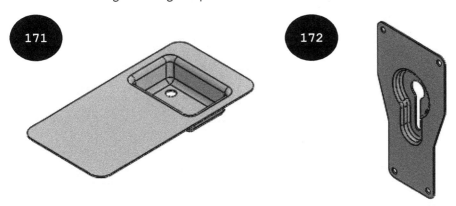

1. Invoke the **Design Library Task Panel** by clicking on the **Design Library** tab in the Task Panel, see Figure 173.

2. Expand the **design library** folder and then the **forming tools** sub-folder in the **Design Library Task Panel**. A list of all available different categories of forming tool parts appears in the expanded **forming tools** sub-folder, refer to Figure 173.

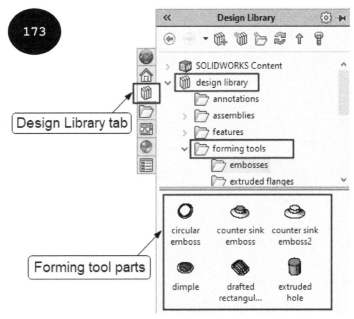

3. Select the required category in it. The forming tool parts that are available in the selected category appear on the lower part of the **Design Library Task Panel**, refer to Figure 173. In this figure, the **embosses** category is selected. As a result, all the forming tools parts that are available in the embosses category appears on the lower part of the **Design Library Task Panel**.

4. Drag and drop the required formed tool part from the lower part of the **Design Library Task Panel** to a face of the sheet metal component in the graphics area, see Figure 174. Also, the **Form Tool Feature PropertyManager**, see Figure 175.

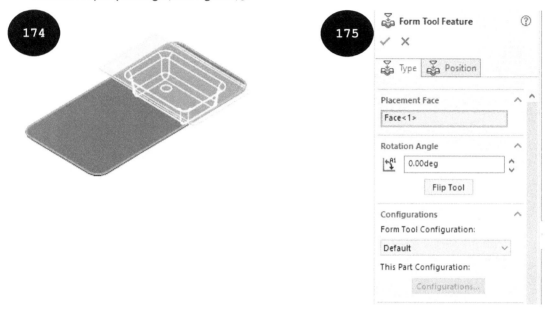

5. Enter the required angle in the **Rotation Angle** field of the PropertyManager for rotating the formed tool part on the selected face of the sheet metal part, if needed. Next, click anywhere in the graphics area. The formed tool gets rotated as per the defined angle of rotation.

6. Click on the **Flip Tool** button in the PropertyManager to flip the direction of formed tool part on the other side of the face selected.

7. Click on the **Position** tab in the PropertyManager then apply the required dimensions or relations to the insertion point of the formed tool part for defining its position on the selected face of the sheet metal component, see Figure 176.

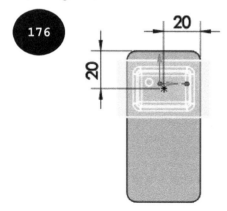

Note: You can also insert multiple sub-instances of the formed tool part by clicking on the selected face of the sheet metal component.

8. After defining the position of the formed tool part on the selected face of the sheet metal component, click on the green tick-mark button. The formed feature gets created, see Figure 177.

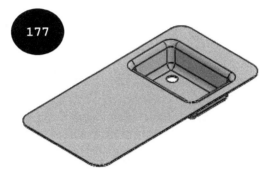

Creating a Vent

In SOLIDWORKS, you can create a vent feature on a face of a sheet metal component by using the **Vent** tool in the **Sheet Metal CommandManager**, see Figure 178. A vent feature uses a closed sketch segment as its boundary and the open or closed sketch segments inside the selected boundary as its ribs and spars, see Figure 178. The method for creating a vent feature is discussed below:

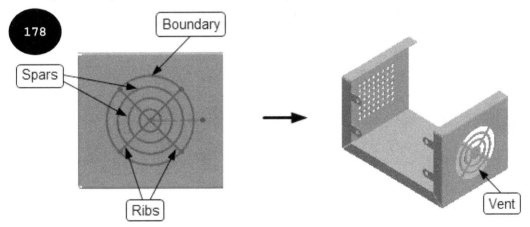

1. Invoke the Sketching environment by selecting a face of the sheet metal component where you want to create a view feature.

2. Create a sketch of the vent feature which includes a closed sketch segment as a boundary and closed or open sketch segments inside the boundary as ribs and spars segments, refer to Figures 178 and 179. Note that you can create a vent of any shape by creating its sketch, accordingly.

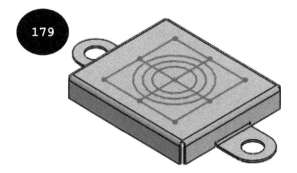

3. After creating the sketch of the vent feature, exit the Sketching environment. Next, click anywhere in the graphics area to exit the current selection set.

4. Click on the **Vent** tool in the **Sheet Metal CommandManager**, see Figure 180. The **Vent PropertyManager** appears, see Figure 181. Also, you are prompted to select a closed sketch segment as the boundary of the vent feature, since the **Boundary** field is activated in the PropertyManager, by default.

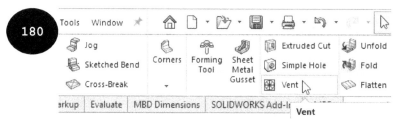

5. Select the sketch segment that forms a closed loop as the boundary of the vent feature, refer to Figure 182. The preview of a vent feature appears such that the material that lies inside the defined boundary gets removed from the face of the sheet metal component. In Figure 182, outer four sketch segments are selected to define the boundary of the vent feature.

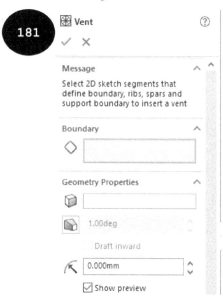

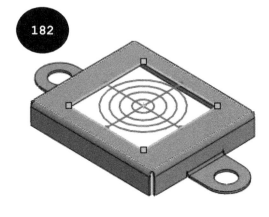

Note: The face of the sheet metal component on which the sketch is created gets selected automatically as the face to create the vent feature and its name appears in the **Select a face on which to place the vent** field of the **Geometry Properties** rollout. If the face on which the vent is to be created is not selected in this field, then the preview of the vent feature will not appear and you need to select the face to create the vent feature, manually.

6. Ensure that the face on which the vent is to be created is selected in the **Select a face on which to place the vent** field of the **Geometry Properties** rollout.

    Draft On/Off: The Draft On/Off button is used for adding draft angle (tapering) to the vent feature. By default, this button is not enabled. As a result, the resultant vent feature is created without having any tapering in it. To add tapering to a vent feature, click on the **Draft On/Off** button. The **Draft Angle** field and the **Draft inward** check box get enabled in the rollout of the PropertyManager. The **Draft Angle** field is used for entering the draft angle for the vent feature and the **Draft inward** check box is used for reversing the direction of the draft.

    Radius for the fillets: The Radius for the fillets field is used for defining the fillet radius at the intersections between the boundary, ribs, and spars of the vent feature, refer to Figures 183 and 184. Figure 183 shows a resultant vent feature without any fillet radius (o fillet radius), whereas Figure 184 shows a resultant vent feature with a fillet radius at the intersections among the boundary, ribs, and spars of the vent feature.

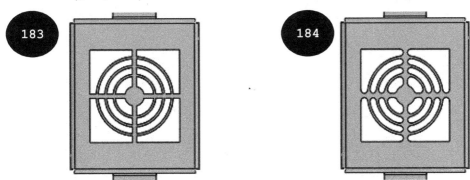

    Show preview: By default, the **Show preview** check box is selected. As a result, while creating a vent feature, its preview appears in the graphics area.

    Flow Area: The Flow Area rollout of the PropertyManager shows the total area available inside the boundary of the vent feature in square units, see Figure 185. It also shows the open area inside the boundary of the vent feature for the air flow in terms of the percentage of the total area. The value of the open area gets updated as you add vent entities such as fillets, ribs, and spars.

Flow Area
Area = 1764.000 square mm
Open area = 90.70 %

7. Click on the **Select 2D sketch segments that represent ribs of the vent** field in the **Ribs** rollout and then select the open or closed sketch segments inside the defined boundary as the ribs of the vent feature, see Figure 186. In this figure, two open sketch segments are selected as ribs.

8. Click on the **Enter the width of the ribs** field in the **Ribs** rollout and then enter the width of the ribs in it.

9. Click on the **Select 2D sketch segments that represent spars of the vent** field in the **Spars** rollout and then select the open or closed sketch segments inside the boundary as the spars of the vent feature, see Figure 187. In this figure, three outer circular sketch segments are selected as spars.

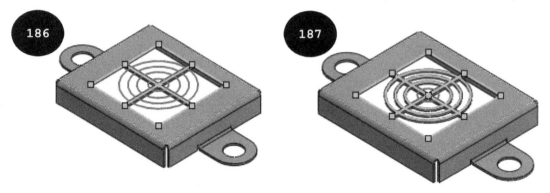

10. Click on the **Enter the width of the spars** field in the **Spars** rollout and then enter the width of the spars in it.

11. Click on the field in the **Fill-In Boundary** rollout and then select a closed sketch segment inside the boundary as the fill-in boundary acting as a supporting boundary for the vent feature, see Figure 188. In this figure, the inner most circle of the sketch is selected as the fill-in boundary.

12. Click on the green tick-mark button in the **Vent PropertyManager**. A vent feature gets created, see Figure 189.

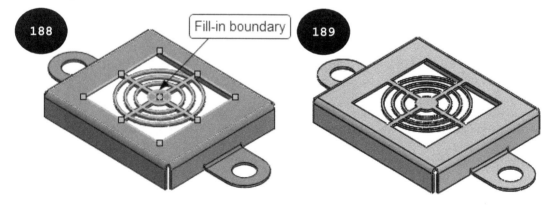

Fill-in boundary

Converting a 3D Solid Part into a Sheet Metal

In SOLIDWORKS, you can also convert a 3D solid part into a sheet metal component by using the **Convert to Sheet Metal** tool, see Figure 190. The method for converting a 3D solid part into a sheet metal component is discussed below:

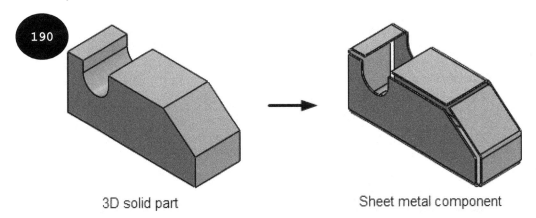

3D solid part   Sheet metal component

1. Create a 3D solid part in the Part modeling environment or open an existing 3D solid part to be converted into a sheet metal component.

Note: To learn creating 3D solid parts, assemblies, and drawings, refer to "**SOLIDWORKS 2021: A Power Guide for Beginners and Intermediate User**" textbook by CADArtifex.

2. Click on the **Convert to Sheet Metal** tool in the **Sheet Metal CommandManager**, see Figure 191. The **Convert to Sheet Metal PropertyManager** appears, see Figure 192. Also, the available 3D solid part becomes transparent in the graphics area.

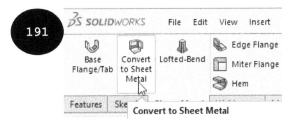

3. Ensure that the **Select a fixed entity** field is activated in the **Sheet Metal Parameters** rollout to select a face of the part as the fixed face of the resultant sheet while creating its flat pattern.

4. Select a face of the 3D solid part as the fixed face of the model that remains fixed when the resultant sheet gets flattened, refer to Figure 193. The selected face gets highlighted in the graphics area and its name appears in the **Select a fixed entity** field in the **Sheet Metal Parameters** rollout. In Figure 193, the bottom face of the 3d solid part is selected as the fixed face.

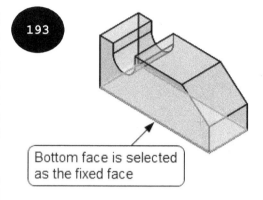

Bottom face is selected as the fixed face

5. Enter the required sheet thickness and the inner bend radius in the **Sheet thickness** and **Default radius for bends** fields of the **Sheet Metal Parameters** rollout, respectively.

   Reverse thickness: The **Reverse thickness** check box is used for reversing the sheet metal thickness direction from inside to outside the part or vice-versa.

   Keep body: The **Keep body** check box is used for keeping the original solid part in the graphics area. By default, this check box is cleared. As a result, the original solid part gets consumed by the resultant sheet metal component.

6. Ensure that the **Keep body** check box is cleared in the **Sheet Metal Parameters** rollout.

7. Click on the **Select edges/faces that represent bends** field in the **Bend Edges** rollout of the PropertyManager for selecting the bend edges of the sheet.

8. Click to select edges of the selected fixed face as the bend edges of the sheet, see Figure 194. The bend edges get selected and the **Radius** callout gets attached to all the edges selected. Also, their corresponding edges get selected automatically as the rip edges and the **Gap** callout attached to them. In Figure 194, all the four edges of the fixed face are selected as the bend edges and their corresponding edges are selected automatically as the rip edges.

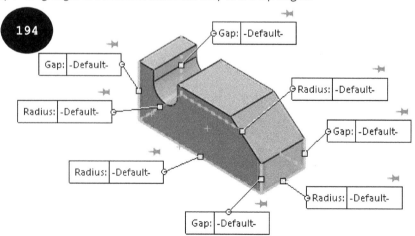

Tip: It is recommended to first select the edges of the fixed face and then continue with the selection of other edges of the part as the bend edges of the sheet.

After selecting the edges of the fixed face as the bend edges, you can also select other edges of the part as the bend edges.

9. Select the other required edges of the part as the bend edges, see Figure 195.

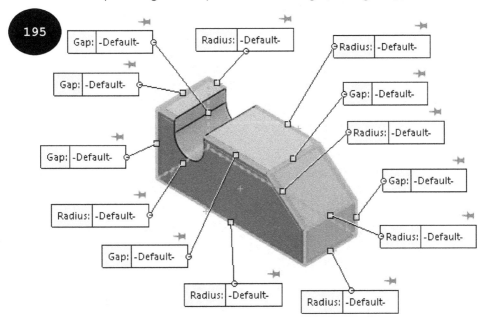

Note: The selected bend edges appear in blue color with Radius callout, whereas the rip (gap) edges appear in pink color with Gap callouts. Also, the name of the selected bend edges appears in the field of the **Bend Edges** rollout and the name of the rip edges appears in the field of the **Rip Edges found (Read-only)** rollout of the PropertyManager.

Show Callouts: By default, the **Show Callouts** check box is selected in the **Bend Edges** and **Rip Edges found (Read-only)** rollouts of the PropertyManager. As a result, the callouts for the bend edges and the rip edges are displayed in the graphics area. Note that the **Default** option is selected in each callout, which indicates that the default specified bend radius and the gap/rip value are used for bend edges and rip edges, respectively. You can edit or change the default bend radius and the rip value of an edge, individually by clicking on the **Default** option of their respective callout in the graphics area.

Collect All Bends: The **Collect All Bends** button in the **Bend Edges** rollout is used for finding all the appropriate bends in the part, automatically. It works better in case of an imported part with pre-existing bends in it.

Rip Sketches: The Select a sketch to add a rip field in the **Rip Sketches** rollout is used for selecting a sketch line or entity to define the required rip on a face of the part.

Corner Defaults: The options in the **Corner Default** rollout are used for defining the default rip type, rip gap, and rip overlap ratio for the corners of the resultant sheet metal component. You can define the rip type by clicking on the required button (**Open Butt**, **Overlap**, or **Underlap**) button in this rollout. The **Default gap for all rips** field is used for specifying the default rip gap for the corners and the **Default overlap ratio for all rips** field is used for specifying the default rip overlap ratio for the corners.

Tip: You can also customize the bend allowance and relief by using the options available in the **Bend Allowance** and **Auto Relief** rollouts of the PropertyManager, respectively. The options in these rollouts are same as discussed earlier.

---

10. Define the rip type, rip gap, and rip overlap ratio in the **Corner Defaults** rollout of the PropertyManager, as required.

11. Click on the green tick-mark button in the PropertyManager. The 3D solid part gets converted to a sheet metal component, see Figure 196.

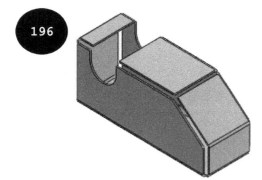

196

Converting a 3D Shelled Part into a Sheet Metal

In SOLIDWORKS, you can convert a 3D shelled part into a sheet metal component by adding rips and bends, see Figure 197. The method for converting a 3D shelled part into a sheet metal component is discussed below:

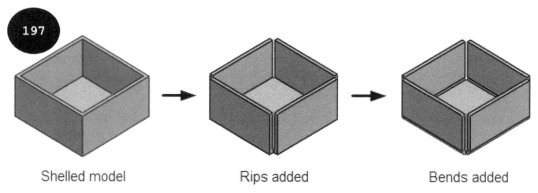

197

Shelled model   Rips added   Bends added

1. Create a 3D shelled model of uniform thickness by removing at least one of the faces of the model in the Part modeling environment, refer to Figure 198.

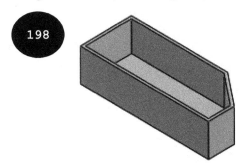

Now, you need convert the shelled model into a sheet metal component by adding rips and bends.

2. Click on the **Rip** tool in the **Sheet Metal CommandManager**, see Figure 199. The **Rip PropertyManager** appears, see Figure 200. Also, you are prompted to select edges of the shelled model to be ripped, since the **Edges to Rip** field is activated in the PropertyManager, by default.

3. Click to select the internal or external edges of the model to be ripped, see Figure 201. Two arrows appear on each selected edge of the model indicating that the rips are added on both the directions. In this figure, outer five edges are selected.

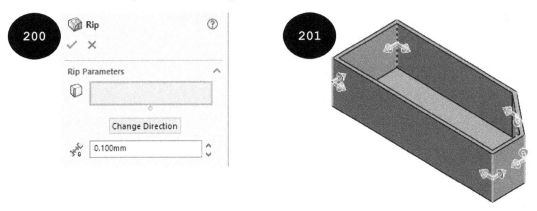

Change Direction: The Change Direction button is used for changing the rip direction of the selected edge sequences from one direction, to the other direction, and then to both directions.

To do so, you need to first select the name of the edge in the **Edges to Rip** field whose rip direction is to be changed and then click on the **Change Direction** button in the PropertyManager.

4. Change the rip directions for the selected edges by clicking on the **Change Direction** button, if needed, as discussed above.

5. Enter the required gap distance value in the **Rip Gap** field of the PropertyManager.

6. Click on the green tick-mark button in the PropertyManager. The rips of defined gap value are added to the selected edges of the model, see Figure 202.

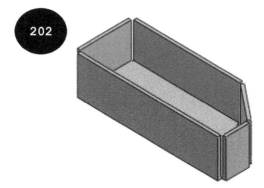

Now, you need to add bends on the model to make it a sheet metal component.

7. Click on the **Insert Bends** tool in the **Sheet Metal CommandManager**, see Figure 203. The **Bends PropertyManager** appears, see Figure 204. Also, you are prompted to select a fixed face of the model that remains fixed when the resultant sheet gets flattened, since the **Fixed Face or Edge** field is activated in the PropertyManager, by default.

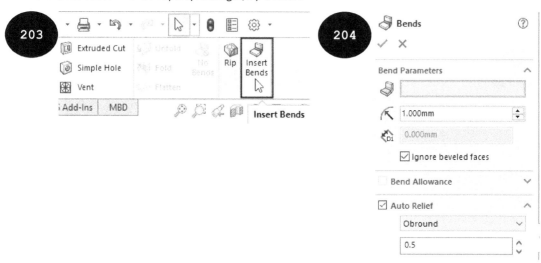

8. Click on select a fixed face of the model, see Figure 205. The face gets highlighted and its name appears in the **Fixed Face or Edge** field of the PropertyManager.

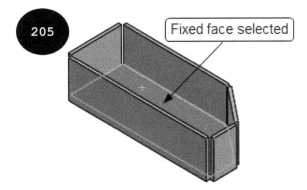

Fixed face selected

9. Enter the required bend radius in the **Bend Radius** field of the **Bend Parameters** rollout.

Tip: You can also add rips to the edges of a solid model by using the **Rip Parameters** rollout of the **Bends PropertyManager**. The method for adding rips is same as discussed earlier.

10. Accept the remaining default options and then click on the green tick-mark button in the PropertyManager. The **SOLIDWORKS** message window appears, which informs that the auto relief cuts were made for one or more bends. Next, click on the **OK** button in this window. The bends of specified radius are added on all the edges of the selected fixed face, see Figure 206. Also, the **Sheet-Metal** node is added in the **FeatureManager Design Tree**, which indicates that the solid shelled model gets converted to a sheet metal component.

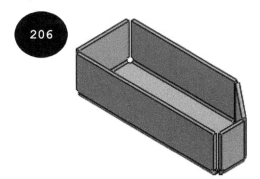

Mirroring and Patterning a Sheet Metal Feature

In SOLIDWORKS, you can mirror and pattern a sheet metal feature by using the **Mirror, Linear Pattern**, and **Circular Pattern** tools of the **Features CommandManager**, respectively in the same manner as of mirroring and patterning a solid part feature while creating a 3D solid part.

Creating a Flat Pattern of a Sheet Metal Part

In a tool room or machine shop, the most important thing that you need before creating a sheet metal part/component is the flat pattern layout of the sheet. It defines the shape and size of the raw sheet before it is formed. It also helps in defining the manufacturing process for creating the finished sheet metal component.

In SOLIDWORKS, after creating a sheet metal component, you can generate its flat pattern. To do so, click on the **Flatten** tool in the **Sheet Metal CommandManager**, see Figure 207. The flat pattern layout of the sheet metal component gets generated in the graphics area, see Figure 208. Note that it is a toggle tool. You can click on this tool again for switching back to the sheet metal component.

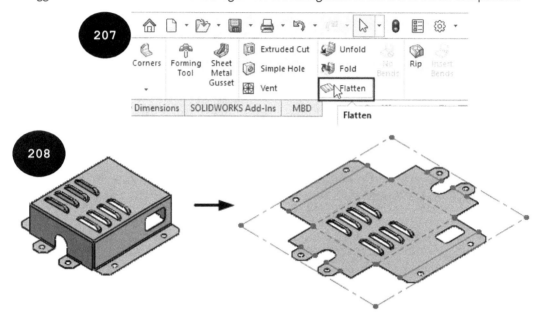

Alternatively, expand the **Flat-Pattern** node available at the end of all features in the **FeatureManager Design Tree**, see Figure 209. Next, click on the **Flat-Pattern1** feature in it and then click on the **Unsuppress** tool in the Pop-up toolbar that appears, see Figure 209. The **Flat-Pattern1** feature gets unsuppress and the flat pattern layout of the sheet metal component gets generated in the graphics area. Similarly, you can suppress the **Flat-Pattern1** feature for switching back to the sheet metal component.

Flattening Selected Bends of a Sheet Metal Part

In SOLIDWORKS, you can unfold or flatten selected bends (one, more than one, or all bends) of a sheet metal component. To do so, click on the **Unfold** tool in the **Sheet Metal component**, see Figure 210. The **Unfold PropertyManager** appears, see Figure 211. Also, you are prompted to select a fixed face of the sheet metal component that will remain fixed in the resultant flat pattern, since the **Fixed Face** field is activated in the PropertyManager, by default.

Click to select a face of the sheet metal component as the fixed face in the graphics area, see Figure 212. After selecting the fixed face, the **Bends to unfold** field gets activated in the PropertyManager for selecting the bends to be flattened. Select the bends of the sheet metal component to be flattened, see Figure 212. You can select one, more than one, or all the bends of the component to be flattened. In Figure 212, two bends are selected to be flattened. Note that to select all the bends of the sheet metal component, you need to click on the **Collect All Bends** button in the PropertyManager. After selecting the fixed face and bends to be flattened, click on the green tick-mark button in the PropertyManager. The selected bends get flattened, see Figure 213.

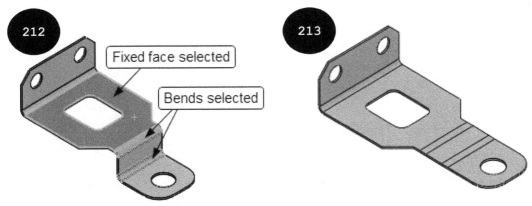

Folding Selected Bends of a Sheet Metal Part

In SOLIDWORKS, you can fold the selected unfolded or flattened bends of a sheet metal component. To do so, click on the **fold** tool in the **Sheet Metal component**, see Figure 214. The **fold** PropertyManager appears and the fixed face of the sheet metal component gets selected automatically in its **Fixed face** field, see Figure 215. Also, you are prompted to select bends to be folded, since the **Bends to fold** field is activated in the PropertyManager, by default.

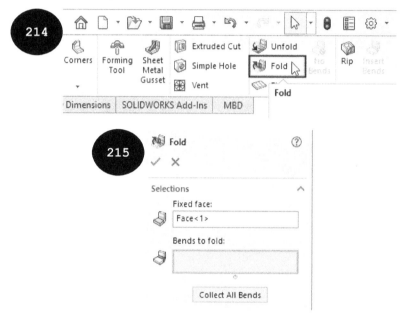

Select the unfolded or flattened bends of the sheet metal component to be folded in the graphics area, see Figure 216. You can select one, more than one, or all the unfolded bends of the component to be folded. In Figure 216, two unfolded bends are selected to be folded. Note that to select all the unfolded bends of the sheet metal component, you need to click on the **Collect All Bends** button in the PropertyManager. Next, click on the green tick-mark button in the PropertyManager. The selected bends get folded in the graphics area, see Figure 217.

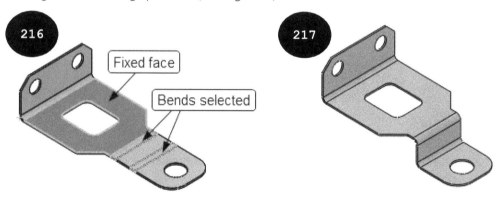

Creating Cuts Across the Bends

To create cuts across the bends of a sheet metal component, you first need to unfold or flatten the bends of the sheet metal component using the **Unfold** tool. After unfolding the bends, you can create cut features across the bends, as required by using the **Extruded Cut** tool, see Figure 218. In this figure, all three bends of a sheet metal component get unfolded by using the **Unfold** tool and the cut feature is created on two of the unfolded bends.

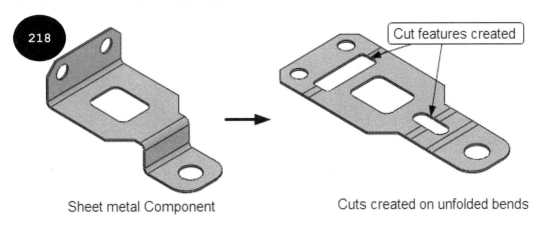

Sheet metal Component   Cuts created on unfolded bends

After creating the cut feature on the unfolded bends of the sheet metal component, fold the bends by using the **Fold** tool, see Figure 219. The cut features are created across the bends of the sheet metal component.

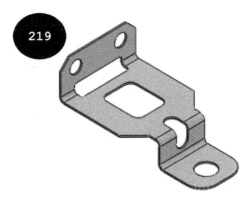

Defining Sheet Parameters to a Custom Material

In SOLIDWORKS, you can define the sheet metal parameters to a custom material of a part document and link these parameters with a sheet metal component. For doing so, invoke a new part document of SOLIDWORKS and then right-click on the **Material < not specified >** option in the **FeatureManager Design Tree**, see Figure 220. A shortcut menu appears. In this shortcut menu, click on the **Edit Material** option. The **Material** dialog box appears, see Figure 221.

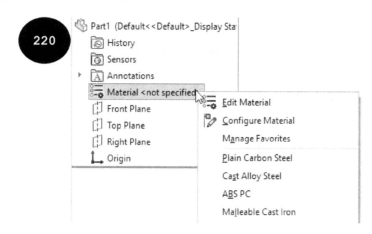

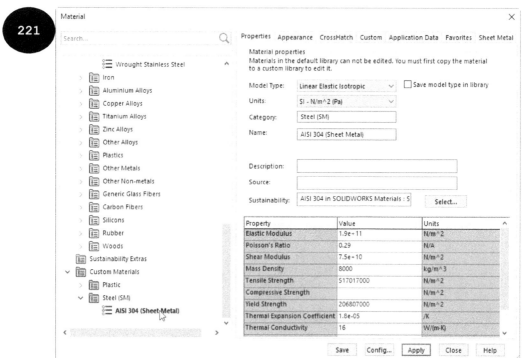

In the **Material** dialog box, create a custom material in the **Custom Materials** category, refer to Figure 221. In this figure, a custom material name **AISI 304 (Sheet Metal)** is created in the **Steel (SM)** category of the **Custom Materials** library.

Note: To create a custom material, you can also copy a standard material from the SOLIDWORKS **Materials** library and paste it inside the **Custom Materials** library of the **Material** dialog box. Next, edit its material properties, as required. To learn more about creating a new material category, custom material, and so on, refer to "**SOLIDWORKS 2021: A Power Guide for Beginners and Intermediate User**" textbook by CADArtifex.

After creating a custom material, select it and then click on the **Sheet Metal** tab in the **Material** dialog box, see Figure 222. The different methods for defining the sheet metal parameters to the selected custom material appears in the dialog box. Select the required radio button (**Gauge Table, Bend Table,** or **Bend Calculation Table**) as a method for defining the sheet metal parameters to the selected custom material. Depending upon the radio button chosen, select the required gauge table, bend table, or bend calculation table, respectively in the drop-down list that is enabled in the dialog box for defining the sheet metal properties. You can also select the **Thickness Range** radio button and then define the bend allowance, bend deduction, or k-factor values for the different sheet metal thickness range in the table that is enabled in the dialog box, refer to Figure 222. In this figure, the bend allowance values are defined for sheet metal thickness ranging from 0 to 6 in different rows of the table. Note that the thickness range specified in the different rows of table must be continuous.

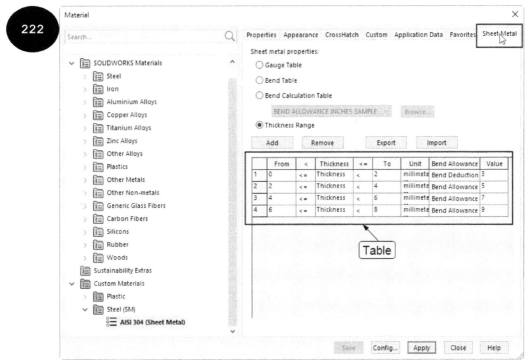

Note: You can use the **Add** button in the dialog box for adding a new row and the **Remove** button for removing a selected row in the table. You can also export the defined table with thickness range values in an excel spreadsheet by using the **Export** button. The **Import** button is used for importing an existing excel spreadsheet containing thickness range values in the table.

After defining the sheet metal parameters to a selected custom material, click on the **Apply** button and then **Close** button in the dialog box. The sheet metal parameters are defined for the custom material. Now, you can use these parameters while creating a sheet metal component. For example, to use the sheet metal parameters defined to a custom material while creating a base flange, select the **Use material sheet metal parameters** check box in the **Base Flange PropertyManager**, see Figure 223.

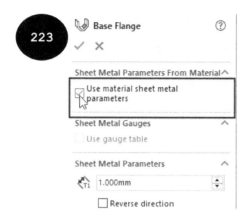

Generating a Drawing View of the Flat Pattern

After creating a sheet metal component, you can generate its flat pattern drawing view in the Drawing environment. To do so, invoke the Drawing environment by selecting the required sheet size, see Figure 224. Note that in the Drawing environment, the **Model View PropertyManager** appears to the left of the sheet.

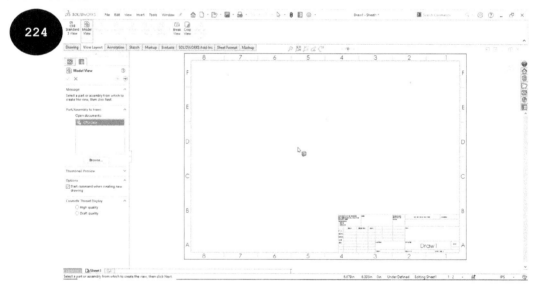

After invoking the Drawing environment, click on the **Browse** button in the **Part/Assembly to Insert** rollout of the **Model View PropertyManager**. The **Open** dialog box appears. Next, browse to the location where the sheet metal component, whose flat pattern view is to be generated, has been saved and then select it. Next, click on the **Open** button in the dialog box. A rectangular box representing the drawing view of the selected component is attached to the cursor. Also, the options of the PropertyManager gets modified, see Figure 225.

Note: If the sheet metal component is listed or available in the **Open documents** field of the **Model View PropertyManager**, then you can double-click on it for generating its flat pattern view. Note that the **Open document** field displays only those components that are opened in the current session of SOLIDWORKS.

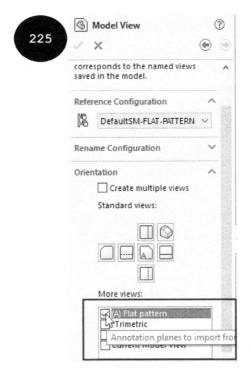

In the modified **Model View PropertyManager**, select the **Flat pattern** check box in the **Orientation** rollout, refer to Figure 225. Next, click to define the placement point of the drawing view on the sheet. The flat pattern drawing view of the selected sheet metal component gets generated, see Figure 226.

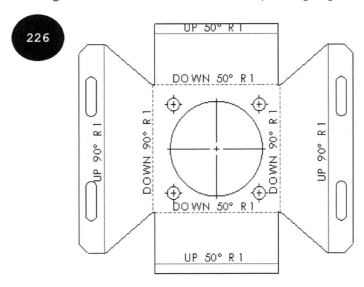

Tutorial 1

Create the sheet metal component shown in Figure 227. The different views, dimensions, and flat pattern of the sheet metal component are shown in Figure 228. All dimensions are in mm.

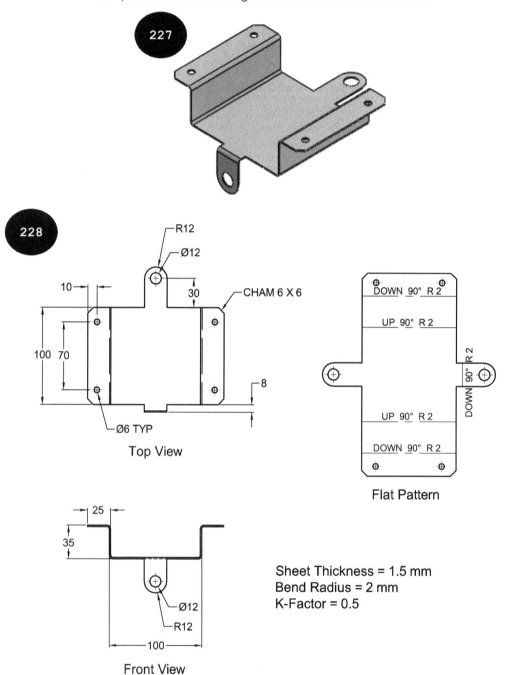

Sheet Thickness = 1.5 mm
Bend Radius = 2 mm
K-Factor = 0.5

Section 1: Invoking the Part Modeling Environment

1. Start SOLIDWORKS by double-clicking on the SOLIDWORKS icon on your desktop. The startup user interface of SOLIDWORKS appears along with the **Welcome** dialog box, see Figure 229.

2. Click on the **Part** button in the **Welcome** dialog box. The Part modeling environment is invoked.

> **Note:** If SOLIDWORKS is already open and the **Welcome** dialog box does not appear on the screen, then you can invoke the **Welcome** dialog box by clicking on the **Welcome to SOLIDWORKS** tool in the **Standard** toolbar or by pressing the CTRL + F2 keys. Alternatively, click on the **New** tool in the **Standard** toolbar and then double-click on the **Part** button in the **New SOLIDWORKS Document** dialog box that appears for invoking the Part modeling environment.

Section 2: Specifying Unit Settings

1. Move the cursor toward the lower right corner of the screen over the Status Bar and then click on the **Unit System** area, see Figure 230. The **Unit System** flyout appears.

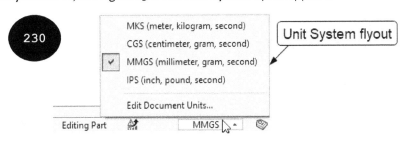

2. Ensure that the **MMGS (millimeter, gram, second)** option is tick-marked in the flyout as the unit system for the current part document.

Section 3: Creating the Base Flange of the Sheet Metal Component
Now, you need to create the base flange of the sheet metal component.

1. Click on the **Sheet Metal** tab in the CommandManager. The tools of the **Sheet Metal CommandManager** appear, see Figure 231.

Note: If the **Sheet Metal** tab is not available in the CommandManager then right-click anywhere on the CommandManager. Next, click on the **Tabs > Sheet Metal** option in the shortcut menu that appears.

---

2. Click on the **Base Flange/Tab** tool in the **Sheet Metal CommandManager** for creating the base flange. The **Message PropertyManager** appears and you are prompted to select either a sketch of the base flange or a sketching plane for creating the sketch. Also, three default planes, which are mutually perpendicular to each other appear in the graphics area.

3. Click to select the Top plane as the sketching plane in the graphics area for creating the sketch of the base flange. The Sketching environment gets invoked and the Top plane becomes normal to the viewing direction.

4. Create the sketch of the base flange in the drawing area by using the sketching tools, see Figure 232.

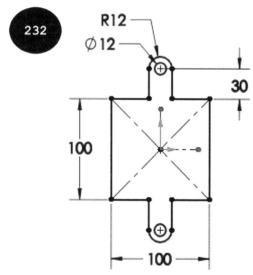

5. After the sketch of the base flange, exit the Sketching environment. The **Base Flange PropertyManager** appears, see Figure 233. Also, the preview of the base flange with default thickness appears in the graphics area.

    Now, you need to define the sheet metal parameters in the **Base Flange PropertyManager** and the same will be used as the default parameters for the entire sheet metal component.

6. Enter **1.5** mm in the **Thickness** field of the **Sheet Metal Parameters** rollout as the thickness of the sheet metal component.

7. Select the **K-Factor** option in the **Bend Allowance Type** drop-down list of the **Bend Allowance** rollout for defining the bend allowance of the sheet metal component in the bent regions.

8. Enter **0.5** as the K-factor value in the **K-Factor** field of the **Bend Allowance** rollout.

9. Select the **Rectangular** option in the **Auto Relief Type** drop-down list of the **Auto Relief** rollout of the PropertyManager.

10. Ensure that the **Use relief ratio** check box is selected and **0.5** value is entered in the **Ratio** field of the **Auto Relief** rollout of the PropertyManager.

11. Click on the green tick-mark button in the PropertyManager. The base flange of the sheet metal component gets created, see Figure 234. Also, the **Sheet-Metal, Base-Flange1**, and **Flat-Pattern** nodes gets added in the **FeatureManager Design Tree**, see Figure 235.

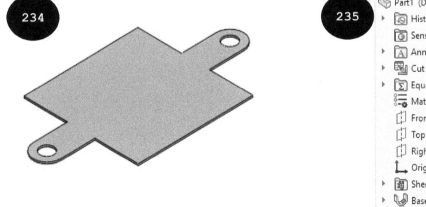

> **Note:** The **Sheet-Metal** node contains all the default sheet metal parameters such as material thickness, bend allowance, and relief that are specified while creating the base flange of the sheet metal component. These parameters gets automatically assigned to all the remaining flanges or features of the sheet metal component as default parameters.
>
> Since the base feature created above does not contain any bends, the bend radius for the sheet metal component is not defined while creating it. In such a case, you need to edit the **Sheet-Metal** node of the **FeatureManager Design Tree** for defining the default bend radius, as required.

Section 4: Editing the Sheet Metal Parameters

Now, you need to edit the sheet metal parameters for defining the default bend radius to 2 mm.

1. Click on the **Sheet-Metal** node in the **FeatureManager Design Tree** and then click on the **Edit Feature** tool in the Pop-up toolbar that appears, see Figure 236. The **Sheet-Metal PropertyManager** appears.

2. Enter **2** mm in the **Bend Radius** field of the **Bend Parameters** rollout in the **Sheet-Metal PropertyManager** as the default bend radius of the sheet metal component, see Figure 237.

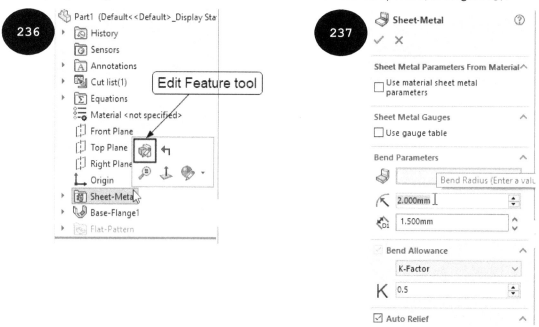

3. Click on the green tick-mark button in the PropertyManager. The default bend radius gets defined.

Section 5: Creating the Edge Flange

Now, you need to create edge flanges of the sheet metal component.

1. Click on the **Edge Flange** tool in the **Sheet Metal CommandManager**, see Figure 238. The **Edge-Flange PropertyManager** appears, see Figure 239. Also, you are prompted to select an edge of a planar face to create the edge flange, since the **Edge** field is activated in the PropertyManager, by default.

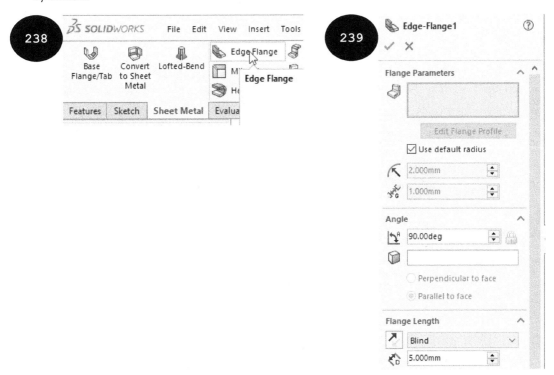

2. Click to select the upper right edge of the base flange in the graphics area, see Figure 240. The preview of an edge flange appears along the entire length of the selected edge, see Figure 240. Also, the name of the selected edge appears in the **Edge** field of the **Flange Parameters** rollout.

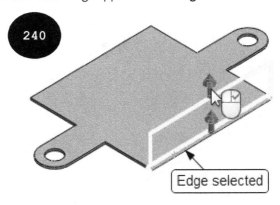

Edge selected

3. Move the cursor upward and then click to define the length of the edge flange arbitrarily in the graphics area.

4. Ensure that **90** degrees is specified as the angle of the edge flange in the **Flange Angle** field of the **Angle** rollout.

5. Ensure the **Blind** option is selected in the **End Condition** drop-down list of the **Flange Length** rollout.

6. Enter **35** mm in the **Length** field of the **Flange Length** rollout as the length of the edge flange.

7. Click to select the **Outer Virtual Sharp** button in the **Flange Length** rollout for measuring the length of the flange from the outer virtual sharp, see Figure 241.

8. Ensure that the **Material Inside** button is activated in the **Flange Position** rollout for adding the flange thickness inside the maximum limit of the sheet, see Figure 241.

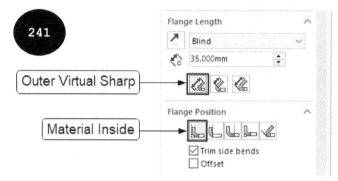

9. Click to select the upper left edge of the base flange for creating an another edge flange of same parameters, see Figure 242. The preview of an another edge flange appears in the graphics area.

10. Click on the green tick-mark button in the PropertyManager. The edge flange feature is created with two edge bends and the same is added in the FeatureManager Design Tree. Figure 243 shows the sheet metal component after creating the edge flange feature.

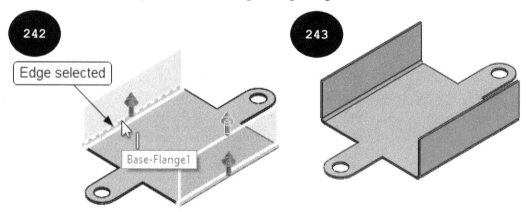

Section 6: Creating the Second Edge Flange Feature

Now, you need to create another edge flange feature on the edges of the previously created flanges.

1. Click on the **Edge Flange** tool in the **Sheet Metal CommandManager**. The **Edge-Flange PropertyManager** appears. Also, you are prompted to select an edge of a planar face to create the edge flange.

2. Select an edge of the previously created right edge flange in the graphics area, see Figure 244. The preview of an edge flange appears along the entire length of the selected edge.

3. Move the cursor towards the right and then click to define the length of the edge flange arbitrarily in the graphics area.

4. Ensure that the **Blind** option is selected in the **End Condition** drop-down list of the **Flange Length** rollout.

5. Enter **25** mm in the **Length** field of the **Flange Length** rollout as the length of the edge flange.

6. Ensure that **90** degrees is specified as the angle of the edge flange in the **Flange Angle** field of the **Angle** rollout.

7. Click on the **Outer Virtual Sharp** button in the Flange Length rollout for measuring the length of the flange from the outer virtual sharp.

8. Ensure that the **Material Inside** button is activated in the **Flange Position** rollout for adding the flange thickness inside the maximum limit of the sheet.

9. Select an edge of the previously created left edge flange in the graphics area, see Figure 245. The preview of an another edge flange with the same parameters appears in the graphics area.

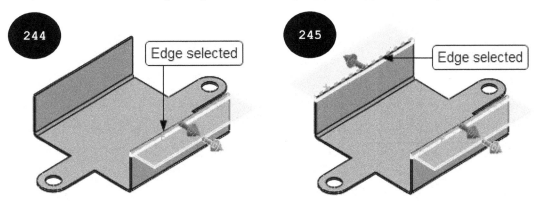

10. Click on the green tick-mark button in the PropertyManager. The second edge flange feature is created with two edge bends and the same is added in the FeatureManager Design Tree. Figure 246 shows the sheet metal component after creating the second edge flange feature.

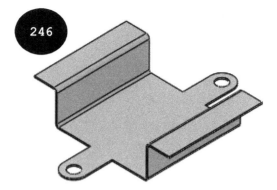

Section 7: Creating the Sketched Bend

Now, you need to create a sketched bend by using a sketch line as the bending line.

1. Click on the **Sketched Bend** tool in the **Sheet Metal CommandManager** for creating a sketched bend, see Figure 247. The **Message PropertyManager** appears and you are prompted to either select a sketching plane for creating the sketch of the bending line or an existing sketch.

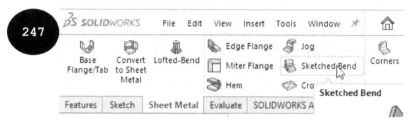

2. Select the top planar face of the base flange in the graphics area for creating the sketch of the bending line, see Figure 248. The Sketching environment gets invoked and the top planar face becomes normal to the viewing direction.

3. Create a line as the bending line for creating the sketched bend in the graphics area, see Figure 249.

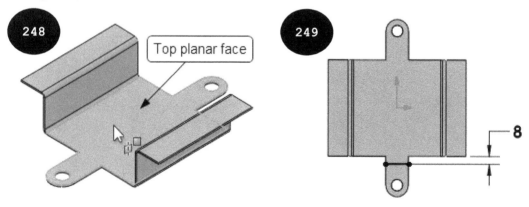

4. After creating the bending line, exit the Sketching environment by clicking on the **Exit Sketch** tool in the **Sketch CommandManager**. The **Sketched Bend PropertyManager** appears, see Figure 250. Also, you are prompted to specify a planar face to be fixed when creating the bend.

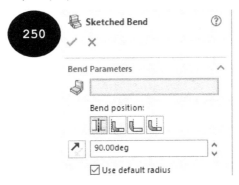

Tip: You can create the bending line before or after invoking the **Sketched Bend** tool.

---

5. Change the orientation of the model to isometric and then select the fixed face of the sheet, see Figure 251. The preview of the sketched bend appears in the graphics area, see Figure 252.

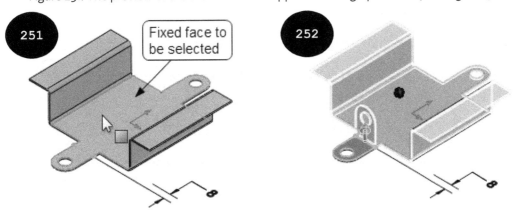

6. Click on the **Material Inside** button in the **Bend position** area of the **Bend Parameters** rollout for adding the material thickness inside the maximum limit of the sheet.

7. Ensure that **90** degrees is specified in the **Bend Angle** field of the PropertyManager.

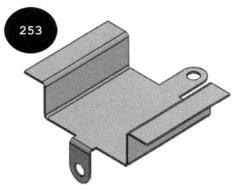

8. Click on the **Reverse Direction** button ↗ in the PropertyManager to reverse the direction of bend to the downward direction.

9. Click on the green tick-mark button in the PropertyManager. A sketched bend is created, see Figure 253.

Section 8: Breaking Corners by Creating Chamfers

Now, you need to break the corner edges of the edge flanges by creating chamfers.

1. Click on **Corners > Break-Corner/Corner-Trim** in the **Sheet Metal CommandManager**, see Figure 254. The **Break Corner PropertyManager** appears.

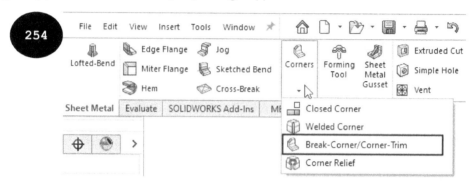

2. Select the four corner edges of the second edge flange feature in the graphics area. The preview of chamfers or fillets appears on the selected edges depending upon whether the **Chamfer** or **Fillet** button is activated in the **Break type** area of the **Break Corner PropertyManager**, see Figure 255. In the figure, the preview of chamfers appears on the selected edges.

3. Click on the **Chamfer** button ⬡ in the **Break type** area of the PropertyManager for creating chamfers on the selected edges.

4. Enter **6** mm in the **Distance** field of the PropertyManager.

5. Click on the green tick-mark button in the PropertyManager. The chamfers are created on the selected corners, see Figure 256.

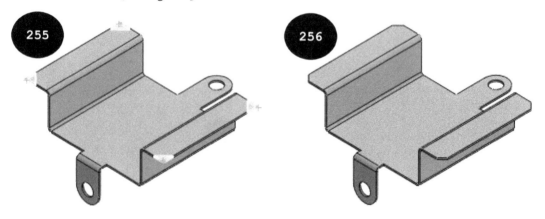

Section 9: Creating the Extruded Cut Feature

Now, you need to create the extruded cut feature on the top planar face of the edge flange.

1. Click on **Extruded Cut** tool in the **Sheet Metal CommandManager**, see Figure 257. The **Extrude PropertyManager** appears.

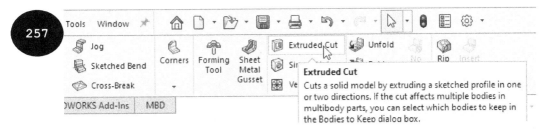

2. Select the top planar face of the edge flange as the sketching plane, see Figure 258. The Sketching environment gets invoked and the selected face becomes normal to the viewing direction.

3. Create four circles of equal diameter as the sketch of the cut feature, see Figure 259.

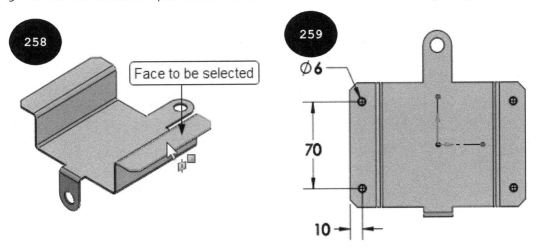

4. After creating the sketch, exit the Sketching environment. The **Cut-Extrude PropertyManager** appears. Also, the preview of the cut feature appears in the graphics area.

5. Change the orientation of the part to isometric.

6. Ensure that the **Link to thickness** check box is selected in the PropertyManager for linking the depth of the cut feature with the sheet thickness.

7. Click on the green tick-mark button in the PropertyManager. The extrude cut feature gets created, see Figure 260.

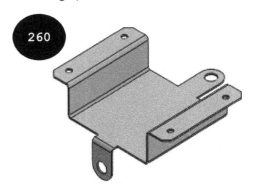

Section 10: Generating the Flat Pattern

Now, you need to create the flat pattern of the sheet metal component.

1. Click on the **Flatten** tool in the **Sheet Metal CommandManager**. The flat pattern of the sheet metal component gets generated in the graphics area, see Figure 261.

2. After reviewing the flat pattern of the sheet metal component, click on the **Flatten** tool again in the **Sheet Metal CommandManager** for switching back to the finished sheet metal component, see Figure 262.

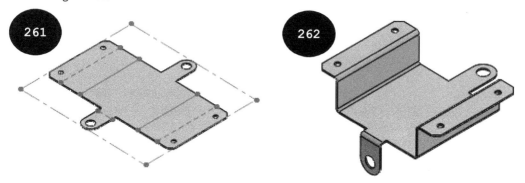

Section 11: Saving the Sheet Metal Component

1. Click on the **Save** tool 🖫 in the **Standard** toolbar. The **Save As** dialog box appears.

2. Browse to the local drive of your system and create a folder with the name **SOLIDWORKS Sheet Metal Design**. Next, double-click on the newly created folder to save the component in it.

3. Enter **Tutorial 1** in the **File name** field of the dialog box and then click on the **Save** button. The sheet metal component is saved with the name Tutorial 1 at the specified location.

Tutorial 2

Create the sheet metal component shown in Figure 263. The different views, dimensions, and flat pattern of the sheet metal component are shown in Figure 264. After creating the component, you need to generate its flat pattern drawing view on the A3 sheet size. All dimensions are in mm.

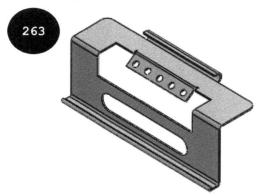

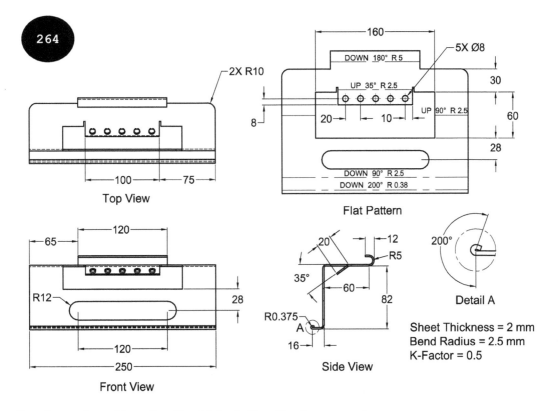

264

Top View

Flat Pattern

DOWN 180° R 5
UP 35° R 2.5
UP 90° R 2.5
DOWN 90° R 2.5
DOWN 200° R 0.38

5X Ø8

2X R10

160
100
75

Front View

120
65
R12
28
120
250

Side View

35°
60
82
16
R0.375
A

Detail A

200°

Sheet Thickness = 2 mm
Bend Radius = 2.5 mm
K-Factor = 0.5

Section 1: Invoking the Part Modeling Environment

1. Start SOLIDWORKS by double-clicking on the SOLIDWORKS icon on your desktop. The startup user interface of SOLIDWORKS appears along with the **Welcome** dialog box.

2. Click on the **Part** button in the **Welcome** dialog box. The Part modeling environment is invoked.

Note: If SOLIDWORKS is already open and the **Welcome** dialog box does not appear on the screen, then you can invoke the **Welcome** dialog box by clicking on the **Welcome to SOLIDWORKS** tool 🏠 in the **Standard** toolbar or by pressing the CTRL + F2 keys.

Section 2: Specifying Unit Settings

1. Move the cursor toward the lower right corner of the screen over the Status Bar and then click on the **Unit System** area, see Figure 265. The **Unit System** flyout appears.

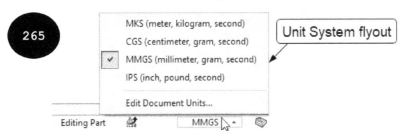

265

Unit System flyout

MKS (meter, kilogram, second)
CGS (centimeter, gram, second)
✓ MMGS (millimeter, gram, second)
IPS (inch, pound, second)

Edit Document Units...

Editing Part   MMGS

2. Ensure that the **MMGS (millimeter, gram, second)** option is tick-marked in the flyout as the unit system for the current part document.

Section 3: Creating the Base Flange

1. Click on the **Sheet Metal** tab in the CommandManager. The tools of the **Sheet Metal** CommandManager appear, see Figure 266.

Note: If the **Sheet Metal** tab is not available in the CommandManager then right-click anywhere on the CommandManager. Next, click on the **Tabs > Sheet Metal** option in the shortcut menu that appears.

---

2. Click on the **Base Flange/Tab** tool in the **Sheet Metal CommandManager** for creating the base flange. The **Message PropertyManager** appears and you are prompted to either select a sketching plane for creating the sketch or an existing sketch. Also, three default planes, which are mutually perpendicular to each other appear in the graphics area.

3. Select the Right plane as the sketching plane in the graphics area for creating the sketch of the base flange. The Sketching environment gets invoked and the Right plane becomes normal to the viewing direction.

4. Create the sketch of the base flange in the drawing area by using the sketching tools, see Figure 267.

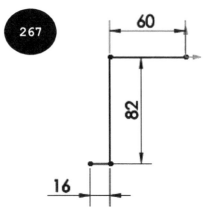

5. After the sketch of the base flange, exit the Sketching environment. The **Base Flange PropertyManager** appears. Also, the preview of the base flange with default thickness appears in the graphics area.

Now, you need to define the sheet metal parameters in the **Base Flange PropertyManager** and the same will be used as the default parameters for the entire sheet metal component.

6. Select the **Mid Plane** option in the **End Condition** drop-down list of the **Direction 1** rollout for defining the depth of the base flange symmetrically about the sketching plane.

7. Enter **250** mm in the **Depth** field of the **Direction 1** rollout as the depth of the base flange. The preview of the base feature appears similar to the one shown in Figure 268.

8. Enter **2** mm in the **Thickness** field of the **Sheet Metal Parameters** rollout as the thickness of the sheet metal component.

9. Enter **2.5** mm in the **Bend Radius** field of the **Bend Parameters** rollout as the default bend radius of the sheet metal component.

10. Select the **K-Factor** option in the **Bend Allowance Type** drop-down list of the **Bend Allowance** rollout for defining the bend allowance of the sheet metal component in the bent regions.

11. Enter **0.5** as the K-factor value in the **K-Factor** field of the **Bend Allowance** rollout.

12. Select the **Rectangular** option in the **Auto Relief Type** drop-down list of the **Auto Relief** rollout of the PropertyManager.

13. Ensure that the **Use relief ratio** check box is selected and then enter **1** in the **Ratio** field of the **Auto Relief** rollout.

14. Click on the green tick-mark button in the PropertyManager. The base flange of the sheet metal component gets created, see Figure 269.

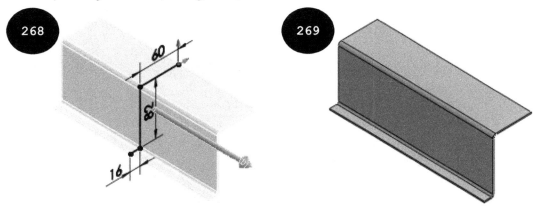

Section 4: Creating the Cut Across the Bend

Now, you need to create the cut feature across the bend of the base flange. Note that for creating a cut across the bend, you first need to unfold or flatten the bend.

1. Click on the **Unfold** tool in the **Sheet Metal CommandManager**, see Figure 270. The **Unfold PropertyManager** appears and you are prompted to select a fixed face.

2. Click on the top planar face of the base flange as the fixed face, see Figure 271. The **Bends to unfold** field gets activated and you are prompted to select bends to be unfolded.

3. Click on the **Collect All Bends** button in the **Unfold PropertyManager**. All the bends get listed in the **Bends to unfold** field of the PropertyManager.

4. Click on the green tick-mark button in the PropertyManager. The selected bends get flattened in the graphics area, see Figure 272.

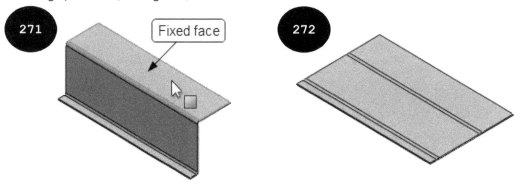

After unfolding the bends, you can create the cut feature across them.

5. Click on the **Extruded Cut** tool in the **Sheet Metal CommandManager** and then select the top face of the flattened sheet as the sketching plane. The Sketching environment gets invoked.

6. Create the sketch of the cut feature in the graphics area, see Figure 273.

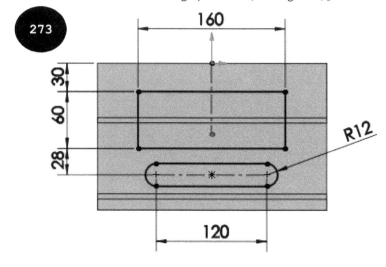

7. After creating the sketch, exit the Sketching environment. The **Cut-Extrude PropertyManager** appears. Next, change the orientation of the component to isometric.

8. Ensure that the **Link to thickness** check box is selected in the PropertyManager for linking the depth of the cut feature with the thickness of the sheet.

9. Click on the green tick-mark button in the PropertyManager. The cut feature is created, see Figure 274.

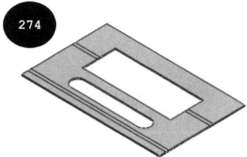

Section 5: Folding the Unfolded Bends of the Sheet

Now, you need to fold the unfolded bends of the sheet metal component.

1. Click on the **Fold** tool in the **Sheet Metal CommandManager**, see Figure 275. The **Fold PropertyManager** appears and the fixed face of the sheet is selected, by default.

2. Click on the **Collect All Bends** button in the PropertyManager. All the unfolded bends get listed in the **Bends to fold** field of the PropertyManager.

3. Click on the green tick-mark button in the PropertyManager. The bends get folded in the graphics area, see Figure 276.

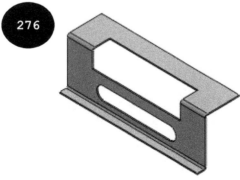

Section 6: Creating the Edge Flange

1. Click on the **Edge Flange** tool in the **Sheet Metal CommandManager**. The **Edge Flange PropertyManager** appears. Also, you are prompted to select an edge.

2. Select the upper edge of the previously created cut feature, see Figure 277. The preview of an edge flange appears along the entire length of the selected edge.

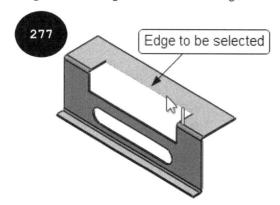

3. Move the cursor downward to a small distance and then click to define the length of the edge flange arbitrarily in the graphics area.

    Now, you need to edit the width of the edge flange along the selected edge.

4. Click on the **Edit Flange Profile** button in the **Flange Parameters** rollout of the PropertyManager. The Sketching environment gets invoked with the display of the **Profile Sketch** dialog box.

5. Drag the side vertical entities of the flange profile (sketch) one by one to adjust the width of the profile similar to the one shown in the Figure 278.

6. Apply dimensions to the flange profile (sketch) in the graphics area, see Figure 279.

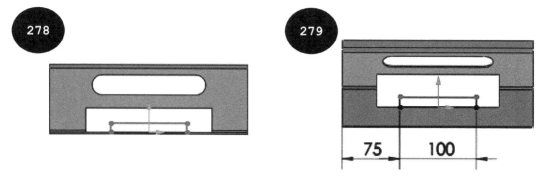

7. After editing the width of the edge flange along the selected edge, click on the **Back** button in the **Profile Sketch** dialog box for switching back to the **Edge Flange PropertyManager** for defining the remaining parameters of the edge flange.

8. Press CTRL + 7 keys to change the orientation of the model to isometric.

9. Enter **35** degrees in the **Flange Angle** field of the **Angle** rollout as the angle of the edge flange.

10. Ensure the **Blind** option is selected in the **End Condition** drop-down list of the **Flange Length** rollout.

11. Enter **20** mm in the **Length** field of the **Flange Length** rollout as the length of the edge flange.

12. Click on the **Outer Virtual Sharp** button in the **Flange Length** rollout for measuring the length of the flange from the outer virtual sharp.

13. Click on the **Material Inside** button in the **Flange Position** rollout for adding the flange thickness inside the maximum limit of the sheet.

14. Click on the green tick-mark button in the PropertyManager. The edge flange feature with specified parameters gets created, see Figure 280.

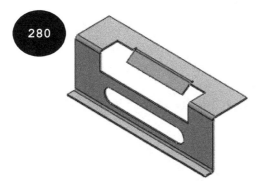

Section 7: Creating the Cut Feature

1. Click on the **Extruded Cut** tool in the **Sheet Metal CommandManager** and then select the top planar face of the previously created edge flange as the sketching plane.

2. Create the sketch of the cut feature (five circles of same diameter and spacing) in the Sketching environment, see Figure 281. Note that you can create one circle and then pattern it to create the remaining instances.

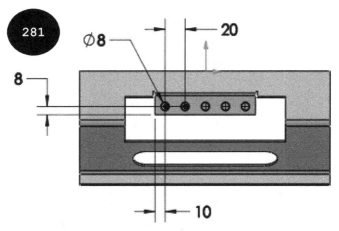

3. After creating the sketch of the cut feature, exit the Sketching environment. The **Cut-Extrude PropertyManager** appears.

4. Ensure that the **Link to thickness** check box is selected in the PropertyManager. Next, press the CTRL + 7 keys to change the orientation of the model to isometric.

5. Click on the green tick-mark button in the PropertyManager. The cut feature gets created, see Figure 282.

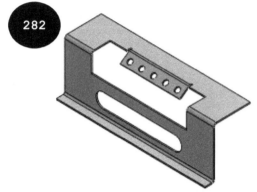

Section 8: Breaking Corners by Creating Fillets

Now, you need to break the corner edges of the edge flanges by creating chamfers.

1. Click on **Corners > Break-Corner/Corner-Trim** in the **Sheet Metal CommandManager**, see Figure 283. The **Break Corner PropertyManager** appears.

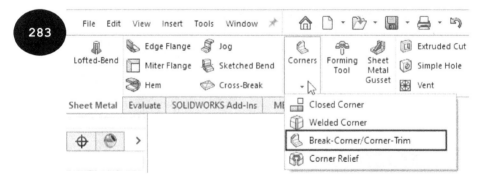

2. Select the upper two corner edges of the sheet metal component in the graphics area, see Figure 284.

3. Click on the **Fillet** button in the **Break type** area of the PropertyManager for creating fillets on the selected edges.

4. Enter **10** mm in the **Radius** field of the PropertyManager.

5. Click on the green tick-mark button in the PropertyManager. The fillets are created on the selected corners, see Figure 285.

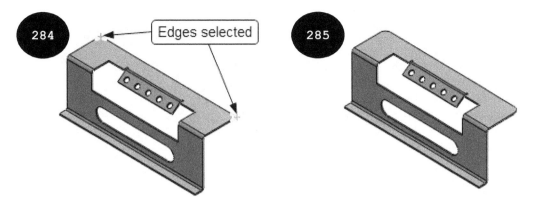

Section 9: Creating Hems

Now, you need to create hems on the edges of the sheet metal component.

1. Click on the **Hem** tool in the **Sheet Metal CommandManager**, see Figure 286. The **Hem PropertyManager** appears. Also, you are prompted to select edges for creating hems.

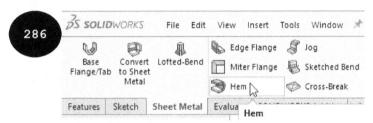

2. Select the upper edge of the sheet metal component for creating the hem, see Figure 287. The preview of the hem appears along the entire length of the selected edge.

3. Click on the **Edit Hem Width** button in the **Edges** rollout of the PropertyManager for editing the width of the hem along the selected edge. The Sketching environment gets invoked with the display of the **Profile Sketch** dialog box.

4. Drag both the open ends of the hem profile one by one to adjust the width of the hem similar to the one shown in Figure 288 and then apply dimensions.

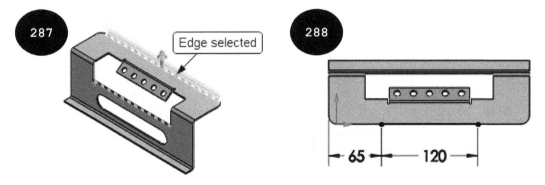

5. After editing the width of the hem, click on the **Back** button in the **Profile Sketch** dialog box to switch back to the **Hem PropertyManager** for defining the remaining parameters of the hem.

6. Press CTRL + 7 keys to change the orientation of the model to isometric.

7. Ensure that the **Bend Outside** button ⊡ is activated in the **Edges** rollout for creating the hem outside the selected edge.

8. Select the **Open** button ⊂ in the **Type and Size** rollout for creating an open hem.

9. Enter **12** mm in the **Length** field and 10 mm in the **Gap Distance** field of the **Type and Size** rollout of the PropertyManager, see Figure 289.

10. Click on the green tick-mark button in the PropertyManager. The hem with specified parameters gets created, see Figure 290.

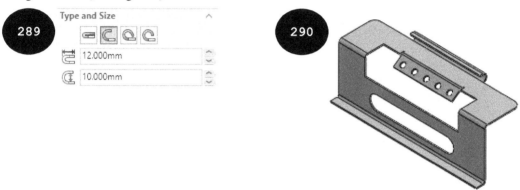

11. Similarly, create tear drop hem of radius **0.375** mm and **200** degrees angle along the entire length of the bottom edge of the sheet metal component, see Figure 291.

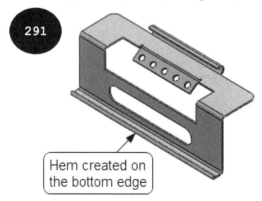

Hem created on the bottom edge

Section 10: Saving the Sheet Metal Component

1. Click on the **Save** tool 🖫 in the **Standard** toolbar. The **Save As** dialog box appears.

2. Browse to the **SOLIDWORKS Sheet Metal Design** folder in the local drive of your system. Note that you need to create this folder if not created earlier.

3. Enter **Tutorial 2** in the **File name** field of the dialog box and then click on the **Save** button. The sheet metal component is saved with the name Tutorial 2 at the specified location.

Section 11: Generating the Flat Pattern Drawing View

Now, you need to generate a drawing view of the flat pattern in the Drawing environment.

1. Click on the **New** tool in the **Standard** toolbar and then double-click on the **Drawing** button in the **New SOLIDWORKS Document** dialog box that appears. The **Sheet Format/Size** dialog box appears.

2. Click on the **New** tool in the **Standard** toolbar and then double-click on the **Drawing** button in the **New SOLIDWORKS Document** dialog box that appears. The **Sheet Format/Size** dialog box appears.

3. Select the **A3 (ANSI) Landscape** sheet size in the **Sheet Format/Size** dialog box and then click on the **OK** button. The Drawing environment gets invoked with the display of the **Model View PropertyManager** on the left of the sheet.

4. Double-click on the **Tutorial 2** component in the **Open documents** filed of the **Part/Assembly to Insert** rollout in the PropertyManager. A rectangular box representing the drawing view of the selected component is attached to the cursor. Also, the options of the PropertyManager get modified.

Note: The **Open document** field displays a list of components that are opened in the current session of SOLIDWORKS. If the component whose drawing view is to be generated is not listed in the **Open documents** field, then you need to click on the **Browse** button for selecting the component whose drawing view is to be generated.

5. Select the **Flat pattern** check box in the **More views** area of the **Orientation** rollout in the modified PropertyManager, see Figure 292.

6. Click to define the placement point of the flat pattern view anywhere on the sheet. The flat pattern view gets generated, see Figure 293. Also, the Projected View PropertyManager appears and the projected view of the flat pattern view appears attached to the cursor.

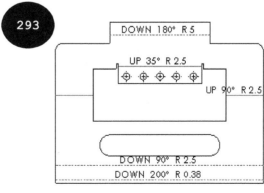

7.   Press the ESC key to exit the placement of the projection views.

Note: If needed, you can create the other drawing views of the sheet metal components on the drawing sheet. To learn about creating different drawing views of a component, refer to "**SOLIDWORKS 2021: A Power Guide for Beginners and Intermediate User**" textbook by CADArtifex.

Section 12: Saving the Flat Pattern Drawing View

1.   Click on the **Save** tool 🖫 in the **Standard** toolbar. The **Save Modified Documents** dialog box appears. In this dialog box, click on the **Save All** button. The **Save As** dialog box appears..

2.   Ensure that the **SOLIDWORKS Drawing (*.drw,*.slddrw)** option is selected in the **Save as type** drop-down list of the dialog box.

3.   Click on the **Save** button in the dialog box. The flat pattern drawing view is saved in the **SOLIDWORKS Sheet Metal Design** folder with the name Tutorial 2.

4.   Save the drawing view in the **SOLIDWORKS Sheet Metal Design** folder of the local drive of your system. Note that you need to create this folder if not created earlier.

Hands-on Test Drive 1

Create the sheet metal component shown in Figure 294. The different views, dimensions, and flat pattern of the sheet metal component are shown in Figure 295. The thickness of the sheet metal component is 1.5 mm, bend radius is 1.5 mm, and K-factor is 0.5. After creating the component, you need to generate its flat pattern. All dimensions are in mm.

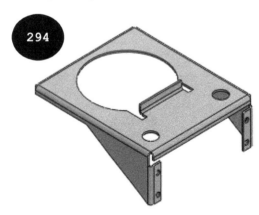
294

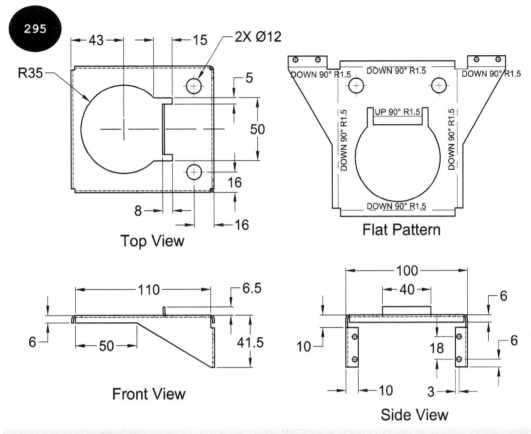

295

Top View

Flat Pattern

Front View

Side View

Hands-on Test Drive 2

Create the sheet metal component shown in Figure 296. The different views, dimensions, and flat pattern of the sheet metal component are shown in Figure 297. The thickness of the sheet metal component is 1.5 mm, bend radius is 2 mm, and K-factor is 0.5. After creating the component, you need to generate its flat pattern drawing view on A3 sheet size. All dimensions are in mm.

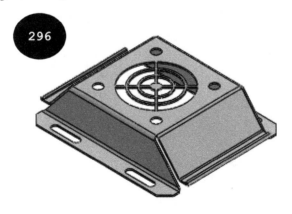

296

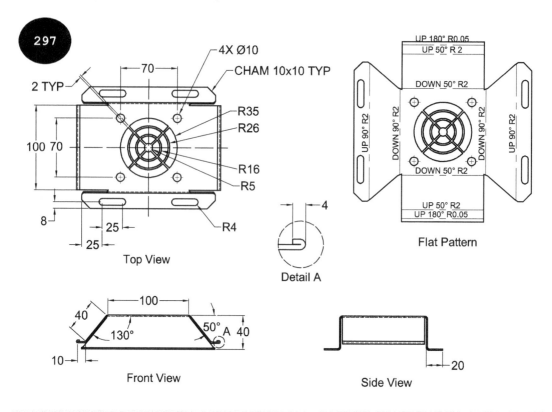

297

4X Ø10
CHAM 10x10 TYP
2 TYP
70
R35
R26
100 70
R16
R5
8
25
25
R4

Top View

Detail A

4

UP 180° R0.05
UP 50° R 2
DOWN 50° R2
UP 90° R2
DOWN 90° R2
DOWN 90° R2
UP 90° R2
DOWN 50° R2
UP 50° R2
UP 180° R0.05

Flat Pattern

100
40
130°
50° A 40
10

Front View

20

Side View

Hands-on Test Drive 3

Create the sheet metal component shown in Figure 298. The different views, dimensions, and flat pattern of the sheet metal component are shown in Figure 299. The thickness of the sheet metal component is 1 mm, bend radius is 2 mm, and K-factor is 0.5. After creating the component, generate its flat pattern layout. All dimensions are in mm.

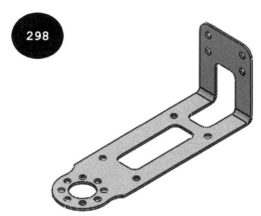

298

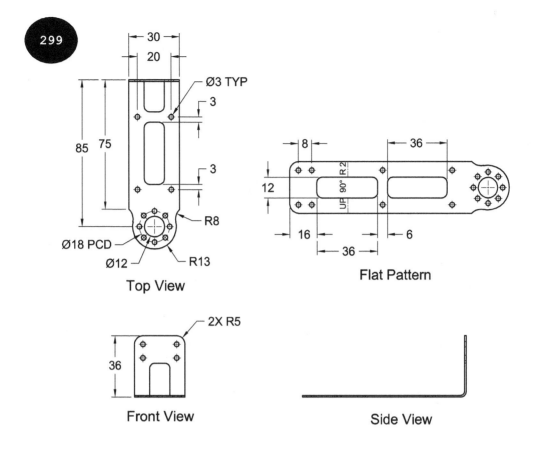

Top View

Flat Pattern

Front View

Side View

Summary

In this book, you have learned the basics of sheet metal design, various sheet metal parameters, and the method for creating a sheet metal component. A detailed discussion is provided on creating a base flange, a tab, a miter flange, a sketched bend, a jog bend, a hem, a lofted bend, an extruded cut, and a vent of a sheet metal component along with discussing closing corners, welding corners, breaking corners of a sheet metal component. The creation and insertion of forming tools is also explained in addition to converting a 3D solid or shelled part into a sheet metal component. Operations such as mirroring, patterning, flattening bends, folding bends, creating cuts across the bends, and generating a flat pattern of a sheet metal component are also discussed. The book also describes methods for defining sheet parameters to a custom material and generating the flat pattern drawing view of a sheet metal component in the Drawing environment.

Questions

- A sheet metal component is a thin and flat piece of metal that has a uniform thickness ranging from _____ to _____ mm.

- The _____ is a bending process in which the punch pushes the sheet into a V-shaped groove of the die for causing it to bend.

- The _____ is a cutting process in which the sheet is divided or cut into two parts by applying a great enough shearing force on the sheet, against the edge of the die, using the punch.

- On selecting the _____ check box, the sheet metal parameters that are defined with the assigned custom material of the current part document will be used for the sheet metal component being created.

- A _____ is simply a Microsoft Excel spreadsheet, which enables you to choose an appropriate sheet metal thickness, based on the material and the gauge numbers.

- A _____ is defined as the ratio between the distance from the neutral axis to the inner bend face and the material thickness.

- In SOLIDWORKS, you can define a _____, _____, or _____ relief type in bend regions to prevent or avoid the unwanted deformation or tear in the sheet metal.

- The _____ node in the FeatureManager Design Tree contains all the default sheet metal parameters such as material thickness, bend radius, bend allowance, and relief that are specified while creating the base flange.

- A flange that is created on an edge of an existing flange of a sheet metal component is known as the _____.

- A _____ flange is a series of flanges created along the existing edges of the sheet metal component.

- A _____ tool is a solid part that acts as a die for creating formed features like embosses, louvers, and lances.

- The _____ tool in the **Sheet Metal CommandManager** is used for generating the flat pattern layout of the sheet metal component.

- In SOLIDWORKS, you can break the corner edges of a sheet metal component by creating chamfers or fillets. (True/False)

- You cannot generate the flat pattern drawing view of a sheet metal component in the Drawing environment. (True/False)

- In a tool room, the most important thing that you need before creating a sheet metal component is the flat pattern layout of the sheet. (True/False)

- In SOLIDWORKS, you can create sheet metal components within the Part modeling environment. (True/False)

INDEX

Other Publications by CADArtifex

SOLIDWORKS Textbooks
SOLIDWORKS 2021: A Power Guide for Beginners and Intermediate User
SOLIDWORKS 2020: A Power Guide for Beginners and Intermediate User
SOLIDWORKS 2019: A Power Guide for Beginners and Intermediate User
SOLIDWORKS 2018: A Power Guide for Beginners and Intermediate User
SOLIDWORKS 2017: A Power Guide for Beginners and Intermediate User
SOLIDWORKS 2016: A Power Guide for Beginners and Intermediate User
SOLIDWORKS 2015: A Power Guide for Beginners and Intermediate User

SOLIDWORKS Simulation Textbooks
SOLIDWORKS Simulation 2021: A Power Guide for Beginners and Intermediate User
SOLIDWORKS Simulation 2020: A Power Guide for Beginners and Intermediate User
SOLIDWORKS Simulation 2019: A Power Guide for Beginners and Intermediate User
SOLIDWORKS Simulation 2018: A Power Guide for Beginners and Intermediate User
Exploring Finite Element Analysis with SOLIDWORKS Simulation 2017

Autodesk Fusion 360 Textbooks
Autodesk Fusion 360: A Power Guide for Beginners and Intermediate Users (4th Edition)
Autodesk Fusion 360: A Power Guide for Beginners and Intermediate Users (3rd Edition)
Autodesk Fusion 360: A Power Guide for Beginners and Intermediate Users (2nd Edition)
Autodesk Fusion 360: A Power Guide for Beginners and Intermediate Users

Autodesk Inventor Textbooks
Autodesk Inventor 2021: A Power Guide for Beginners and Intermediate Users
Autodesk Inventor 2020: A Power Guide for Beginners and Intermediate Users

PTC Creo Parametric Textbooks
Creo Parametric 6.0: A Power Guide for Beginners and Intermediate Users
Creo Parametric 5.0: A Power Guide for Beginners and Intermediate Users

AutoCAD Textbooks
AutoCAD 2021: A Power Guide for Beginners and Intermediate Users
AutoCAD 2020: A Power Guide for Beginners and Intermediate Users
AutoCAD 2019: A Power Guide for Beginners and Intermediate Users
AutoCAD 2018: A Power Guide for Beginners and Intermediate Users
AutoCAD 2017: A Power Guide for Beginners and Intermediate Users
AutoCAD 2016: A Power Guide for Beginners and Intermediate Users

AutoCAD For Architectural Design Textbooks
AutoCAD 2021 for Architectural Design: A Power Guide for Beginners and Intermediate Users
AutoCAD 2020 for Architectural Design: A Power Guide for Beginners and Intermediate Users
AutoCAD 2019 for Architectural Design: A Power Guide for Beginners and Intermediate Users

Exercises Books
A list of exercises books given below:

SOLIDWORKS
SOLIDWORKS Exercises - Learn by Practicing (3 Edition)
SOLIDWORKS Exercises - Learn by Practicing (2 Edition)
SOLIDWORKS Exercises - Learn by Practicing (1 Edition)

AutoCAD
100 AutoCAD Exercises - Learn by Practicing (2 Edition)
100 AutoCAD Exercises - Learn by Practicing (1 Edition)

www.ingramcontent.com/pod-product-compliance
Lightning Source LLC
LaVergne TN
LVHW081346050326
832903LV00024B/1340